21世纪英语专业系列教材·新世纪翻译系列教程

中西文化与汉英翻译文本比较

Contrast of Sino-Western Cultures and Chinese-English Translation Texts

刘宇红　主编

北京大学出版社
PEKING UNIVERSITY PRESS

图书在版编目(CIP)数据

中西文化与汉英翻译文本比较/刘宇红主编. —北京：北京大学出版社，2017. 9
(21 世纪英语专业系列教材 · 新世纪翻译系列教程)
ISBN 978-7-301-28704-0

Ⅰ. ①中… Ⅱ. ①刘… Ⅲ. ①东西文化 – 比较文化 – 文化研究②英语 – 翻译 – 研究 Ⅳ. ①G04 ②H315.9

中国版本图书馆 CIP 数据核字（2017）第 217026 号

书　　名	中西文化与汉英翻译文本比较 ZHONG-XI WENHUA YU HAN-YING FANYI WENBEN BIJIAO
著作责任者	刘宇红　主编
责 任 编 辑	黄瑞明
标 准 书 号	ISBN 978-7-301-28704-0
出 版 发 行	北京大学出版社
地　　址	北京市海淀区成府路 205 号　100871
网　　址	http://www.pup.cn　　新浪微博：@北京大学出版社
电 子 信 箱	zpup@pup.cn
电　　话	邮购部 62752015　发行部 62750672　编辑部 62754382
印 刷 者	天津和萱印刷有限公司
经 销 者	新华书店
	787 毫米 × 1092 毫米　16 开本　11.25 印张　310 千字
	2017 年 9 月第 1 版　2022 年 7 月第 3 次印刷
定　　价	45.00 元

前　言

全书分16章，分别涵盖政治制度、法律、文学、典籍、影视、新闻传播、传统文化、社会流行语、体育、科技、医药、气象、旅游、贸易、动植物、餐饮等16个领域，每一领域成为一章。

在内容安排上，每章包括五节，第一节是解题，介绍该领域的基础知识或基本概念。第二节是该领域的文化对比，介绍中国和西方社会在该领域的差别，对比只限于文化视域，不涉及优劣的评判。英语的民族文化载体主要是英国和美国，所以本书对西方文化的介绍主要针对英美两国，有些章节会涉及它们共同的文化渊源，即古希腊文明和古罗马文明。文化对比服务于语言比较，所以我们将文化对比（第二节）置于语言比较（第三节）之前。

第三节是语言比较，涉及汉语和英语在特定领域的语言使用规律，即相同语义内容的语际表达差异，与翻译技巧直接关联。翻译技巧的介绍不同于经典翻译教材对微观翻译技能的介绍，如长句分译、短句合译、名词转换为动词、动词转换为名词等，本节更重视源于文化价值观与思维传统差异所导致的语言表达差异，比如中国人重视直觉思维、意象思维，坚持天人合一，重视人际和谐，重视对外物的直接把握以及与此相关的整体思维等，以英美人为代表的西方文化与此相对。文化价值观和思维传统的差别在很大程度上影响甚至左右了语言表达和语际翻译。这些方面是每章第三节涉及的内容，该节以特定领域的经典例句为载体，对英汉两种语言在所选定领域的语言差异做了较深入的比较，是对第二节文化差异的呼应和具体化。

第四节和第五节分别是中西文化与汉英语言对比的译例样板和专业词汇对照表。译例样板的选题取自该领域较有代表性的语篇，体现文化差异的典型性特征和语际差异的应对技巧，在译例样板之后是该领域专门词汇和用语的对照列表，比如在第一章政治制度的比较后，我们选择了奥巴马的国情咨文英汉对照文本作为样板，让读者在逐段的对照阅读中体悟两种文化和两种语言的差异；在第二章法律制度的比较后，我们选择了《江苏省劳动合同条例》的英汉逐句对照作为样板，保证读者通过对译例样板的阅读，增强对于文化与语言差异的感性认知和模仿技能。在了解了文化差异、语言差异并接触了译例样板之后，每章的第五节给读者提供一个专业词汇的小型语料库，既备查阅，也可让读者在记诵之后举一反三，加深对于英汉语言与文化差异的敏锐性，提高翻译的准确性和效率。

本书最大的特点是内容全面，知识覆盖面广，涵盖政治、经济、文化、艺术、科技、社会生活、风土人情等各个方面。

本书可以用作文化读本，也可以用作翻译读本，读者面广，适用性大。作为文化读本，本书以专题形式对东西方各领域的差异分别介绍，不以形而上的综述为旨要，而以专题作为知识载体，可以让读者通过特定领域的对比介绍来了解东西方在各领域的文化差异及其历史渊源。作为翻译读本，本书回避了现有翻译教材的高深理论，不以介绍 Nida 和 Newmark 等翻译理论大家的深奥理论为目标，而是把适用于各类文本的翻译技巧以精典的例子为载体，以文化差异的导入为前提，让读者自觉接受英汉两种语言的特点和转换规律。

本书可用于高校本科生通识教育如“中外文化读本”“英汉语比较导论”“语言与文化的互动”等课程的课本，在通识教育成为高校本科生培养的主要特征的前提下，语言与文化的比较是适用于文、理、工各类学生的题材首选。本书以英语为工作语言，可以拓展学生在相关领域的专门词汇，也可以让学生熟悉相关领域和相关内容表达的经典句型，所以本书的每一章都具有专门用途英语(English for Specific Purpose)的特征。

本书也可以用作外语类硕士研究生和翻译专业学位(MTI：Master of Translation and Interpretation)的专业课程“英汉翻译技巧”和“中外文化对比”课程的教材，同时也适用于其他专业研究生的相关公选课。近十年来，各高校外国语学院的研究生培养有了一个根本性的转向，即不以培养语言学和外国文学的学术型硕士为主体目标，而是转向应用型专业学位研究生的培养，即以培养翻译专业学位(MTI)研究生为主要目标(学制也从三年改为两年)。MTI 学生的就业领域涉及社会各个领域，以从事笔译和口译为职业，本书的 16 个专业领域可以让未来的翻译人员提前了解各领域的中外文化对比和语际转换规则。除此之外，本书也可以作为中外文化比较与英汉翻译的工具书，因为每一章的翻译文本样板和专业词汇库可以满足读者在工作和学习中的不时之需。

Contents

Chapter 1 Contrast of Sino-Western Cultures and Chinese-English Translation Texts in the Field of Political System

1.1 What Is Political System

A political system is a framework which defines acceptable political methods within a given society. It is a system of politics and government and is usually comparable with the legal system, economic system, cultural system, and other social systems.

Political system is intimately related to politics which can be formal and informal.

Formal Politics refers to the operation of a constitutional system of government and publicly defined institutions and procedures. Political parties, public policy or discussions about war and foreign affairs would fall under the category of Formal Politics.

Informal Politics is understood as forming alliances, exercising power and protecting and advancing particular ideas or goals. Generally, this includes anything affecting one's daily life, such as the way an office or household is managed, or how one person or group exercises influence over another. Informal Politics is typically understood as everyday politics, hence the idea that "politics is everywhere."

1.2 Cultural Contrast of Political System in China and the West

1.2.1 Political System in China

China's political system is composed of a bundle of aspects.

1. People's Congress System

The people's congress system is China's fundamental political system. The Constitution of the PRC provides that state power belongs to the people. The National people's Congress (NPC) and local people's congresses at all levels are organs representing the people in exercising state power.

The people's congresses have four main functions and powers: legislation, supervision, appointment and removal of officials, and making decisions on major issues.

These functions are a major reflection of the way the Chinese people exercise their power as masters of the state through the people's congress system. Since the Third Plenary Session of the 11th Central Committee of the Communist Party of China (CPC) in 1978, the people's congress system has seen constant improvement and development.

2. Multi-Party Cooperation and Political Consultative System

Multi-party cooperation and political consultation under the leadership of the Communist Party of China constitute the basic party system in China.

China's party system is distinct from the multi-party or two-party systems in Western countries, as well as the one-party system in a few countries. The CPC acts as the ruling party while, under the leadership of the CPC, other parties participate in the discussion and management of state affairs, in cooperation with the CPC. Cooperative relations between the CPC and other parties are based on the principle of "long-term coexistence and mutual supervision, treating each other with full sincerity and sharing weal or woe."

3. The Chinese People's Political Consultative Conference(CPPCC)

The CPPCC exercises the functions of political consultation, democratic supervision, and participating in the administration and discussion of state affairs. The CPC and governments at all levels consult the CPPCC on fundamental policies and important issues in political, economic, cultural and social affairs before a decision is adopted and during the implementation of such decisions, so as to heed and canvass a wide range of opinions.

4. System of Ethnic Regional Autonomy

The system of ethnic regional autonomy is a basic political system of China. Ethnic autonomous areas in China are divided into three levels, namely, autonomous regions, autonomous prefectures and autonomous counties. So far, China has established 155 ethnic autonomous areas, including five autonomous regions, 30 autonomous prefectures and 120 autonomous counties (banners). The Constitution and the Law on Ethnic Regional Autonomy both stipulate that the state is legally obliged to assist ethnic autonomous areas in speeding up their economic and social development.

5. One Country, Two Systems

The key points of the "one country, two systems" policy are that within the PRC, the mainland will continue with its socialist system, while Hong Kong, Macao and Taiwan will maintain the capitalist system. The aim is to achieve peaceful reunification of the country and maintain stability and prosperity in Hong Kong, Macao and Taiwan.

The Chinese Government has pursued to solve the Taiwan issue with the basic principle of "peaceful reunification and one country, two systems." That is, after the reunification, Taiwan's current socio-economic system and its way of life will remain unchanged.

1.2.2 Political System in the West*

The West is a conceptually loose concept. The English language has its origin in Great Britain and substantially developed in the United States, so it is eligible to confine our contrast of Sino-Western culture to the two countries. This principle will be followed throughout this book.

The British political system is headed by a monarchy but essentially the powers of the monarch as head of state, currently Queen Elizabeth II, are ceremonial. The most important practical power is the choice of the Member of Parliament to form a government, but the monarch follows the convention that this opportunity is granted to the leader of the political party with the most seats in the House of Commons or who stands the best chance of commanding a majority in a vote of confidence in the Commons.

The House of Commons is the lower chamber but the one with the most authority. It is chaired by the Speaker. Unlike the Speaker in the US House of Representatives, the post is non-political and indeed, by convention, the political parties do not contest the Parliamentary constituency held by the Speaker.

The House of Lords is the upper chamber but the one with less authority. Its main roles are to revise legislation and keep a check on Government by scrutinizing its activities. Most members of the House of Lords have been what we called hereditary peers. This meant that years ago a king or queen nominated a member of the aristocracy to be a member of the House and, since then, the right to sit in the House has passed through the family from generation to generation. Almost all the other members of today's House of Lords are what we call life peers. This means that they have been chosen by the Queen, on the advice of the Government, to sit in the House for as long as they live, but afterwards no member of their family has the right to sit in the House. Almost 200 are former Members of Parliament. Others are distinguished figures in fields such as education, health and social policy.

In the British political system, almost all legislation is proposed by the Government and much of it comes from promises made in the manifesto of the relevant political party at the last election. At the beginning of each annual session of the Parliament, the main Bills to be considered are announced by the Queen in a speech opening that year's session of Parliament.

All Government Ministers have to be a member of either the House of Commons (most of them) or the House of Lords (the remainder of them) and every Government Department will have at least one Minister in the Lords, so that the Department can speak

* The West here mainly refers to the UK and the USA.

in either House as necessary. The number of Ministers varies from administration to administration, but typically there will be around 120, the 20 or so most senior being Cabinet Ministers.

The most important person in the British political system is the Prime Minister. The official residence of the Prime Minister is at 10 Downing Street in central London and the country residence of the Prime Minister is at Chequers in Buckinghamshire.

The American political system is different in many ways from the British one.

The Declaration of Independence of 1776 and the Constitution of 1789 form the foundations of the United States federal government. The Declaration of Independence establishes the United States as an independent political entity, while the Constitution creates the basic structure of the federal government.

At the heart of the US Constitution is the principle known as "separation of powers." This means that power is spread between three institutions of the state — the executive (President & Cabinet), the legislature (House of Representatives & Senate) and the judiciary (Supreme Court & federal circuits).

The President is the head of the executive branch of the federal government of the United States. The president is both the head of state and the head of government, as well as the military commander-in-chief and chief diplomat.

The President is elected for a fixed term of four years and may serve a maximum of two terms. The President is not elected directly by the voters but by an Electoral College representing each state on the basis of a combination of the number of members in the Senate (two for each state regardless of size) and the number of members in the House of Representatives (roughly proportional to population). The total Electoral College vote is 538. This means that, to become President, a candidate has to win at least 270 electoral votes.

An important feature of the American political system is that the two major parties — the Democrats and the Republicans — hold a system of primaries to determine who will be their candidate in the general election. These primaries are particularly important when it comes to the four-yearly Presidential election.

The House of Representatives is the lower chamber in the bicameral legislature known collectively as Congress. The House consists of 435 members (set in 1911), each of whom represents a congressional district and serves for a two-year term. House seats are apportioned among the states by population according to each decennial (every 10 years) census. Typically a House constituency would represent around 700,000 people.

The Senate is the upper chamber in the bicameral legislature known collectively as Congress. The original intention of the authors of the US Constitution was that the Senate should be a regulatory group, less politically dominant than the House. However, since the mid 19th century, the Senate has been the dominant chamber and indeed today it is perhaps the most powerful upper house of any legislative body in the world. The Senate consists of 100 members, each of whom represents a state and serves for a six-year term (one third of the Senate stands for election every two years).

The Supreme Court is the highest court in the land. Originally it had five members but over time this number has increased. Below the Supreme Court, there is a system of Courts of Appeal, and, below these courts, there are District Courts. Together, these three levels of courts represent the federal judicial system.

The American political system is dominated by two political parties: the Democratic Party and the Republican Party. The Democratic Party is often represented as a donkey, while the Republican Party is featured as an elephant.

1.3 Chinese-English Translation Texts in the Field of Political System

1.3.1 Cross-matching Between Linguistic Ranks

Language units can be of varying sizes in view of linguistic ranks which, along a bottom-up dimension, can be classified into morpheme, word, phrase or word group, clause and clause complex which is more widely known as sentence. Chinese-English contrast of any style of writing, though politics discourse is at stake in this chapter, poses a correspondence law of cross matching between the linguistic ranks, which can be stated explicitly as follows.

Language units of English at a lower rank corresponds, very often, to units one rank higher in Chinese, which can be diagrammed as follows:

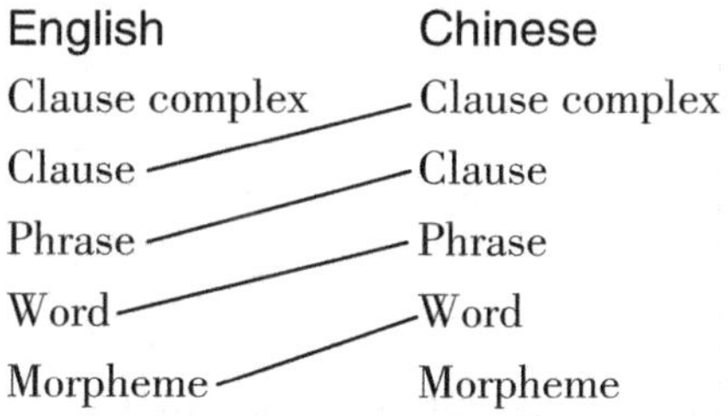

We use the hedge *very often* in the above generalization to indicate that exceptions abound in that there may be horizontal correspondences between the two languages and the lines may go in a more slanting way, that is, a line may link a particular rank in English with a unit two or more ranks higher in the Chinese language.

Let's see examples:

(1) The sanctions would mark the first use of an order signed by President Obama in April establishing the authority to freeze financial and property assets of

individuals and entities overseas who engage in destructive attacks or commercial espionage in cyberspace.

今年 4 月，美国总统奥巴马签署了一项命令，允许冻结从事网络攻击或商业间谍活动的海外个人和团体的金融资产和不动产。

In (1) there are two non-predicate verbal phrases, the past participial phrase *signed by...* and infinitival phrasal *to freeze...*, are rendered into clauses characteristic of the use of predicate verbs, 签署了 and 冻结 respectively.

(2) The United States will not impose economic sanctions on Chinese businesses and individuals before the visit of Chinese President Xi Jinping next week, a senior administration official said Monday.

一名美国高官 14 日表示，在中国国家主席习近平下周访问美国之前，美国不会对中国企业和个人实施经济制裁。

In (2), the prepositional phrase *before the visit of...* corresponds to an adverbial clause of time in Chinese, one rank higher than its source counterpart.

More examples can be found:

(3) Its (her life's) solace was visiting and news.

她平生的慰藉就是探亲访友，打听消息。

In the above example, two words in English correspond to two phrases in Chinese.

(4) She played the piano with skill and passion.

她弹钢琴时技巧娴熟，激情洋溢。

A preposional phrase in English is translated into two juxtaposed clauses in the form of SV.

(5) His fury was exaggerated.

他大发雷霆，未免小题大做。

A word in English corresponds to a verbal phrase in Chinese.

(6) I have a surprise for you.

我有一件你料想不到的事情要告诉你。

One word in English corresponds to a verbal phrase in Chinese.

(7) Ashurst looked, and the poet in him moved.

爱舍斯特注视着，他身上的诗人气质萌动了。

The noun *poet* used figuratively as abstract noun corresponds to a nominal phrase in Chinese.

(8) New price hikes hit Los Angeles supermarketing housewives.

物价一涨再涨，苦了上超市购物的洛杉矶的家庭主妇们。

A noun is linked to a verbal phrase. The plural form of *hike* corresponds to the repetition of the verb 涨 in Chinese.

(9) You might not see one in a hundred with gentleman so plainly written as in Mr Knightley.

莱特立先生的君子风度真是百里挑一。

The noun *gentleman* is used in its figurative sense as *poet* in the preceding example, the corresponding expression 君子风度 is a nominal phrase, very close to the translation of *poet* in (7).

1.3.2 Shortened Form in Chinese Corresponding to Full-length Form in English

The Chinese language is notoriously known for its rich use of shortened expressions by the use of numbers which serves for more brevity but often perplexes readers who lack relevant background information. When translated into English the shortened numerical phrase should be switched into the full lengh form.

Examples can be easily found:

(10) 我们严格落实党中央八项规定精神，持之以恒纠正“四风”。

We have been strictly putting into practice the CPC Central Committee's eight-point decision on improving Party and government conduct and making persistent efforts to $_{1}$fight formalism, $_{2}$bureaucratism, $_{3}$hedonism and $_{4}$extravagance.

(11) 我国发展面临“三期叠加”矛盾。

In its current stage of development, China has to simultaneously $_{1}$deal with the slowdown in economic growth, $_{2}$make difficult structural adjustments and $_{3}$absorb the effects of previous economic stimulus policies.

(12) 逐步实现“三证合一”。

... take gradual steps to integrate $_{1}$the business license, $_{2}$the organization code certificate and $_{3}$the certificate of taxation registration into one certificate.

(13) 统筹实施“四大板块”和“三个支撑带”战略组合。

We will pursue in a coordinated way the strategy of $_{1}$developing the western region, $_{2}$revitalizing the northeast, $_{3}$boosting the rise of the central region, and $_{4}$ensuring the eastern region takes the lead in development and the strategy of developing $_{1}$the Silk Road Economic Belt, the 21st Century Maritime Silk Road, $_{2}$the Beijing-Tianjin-Hebei region, and $_{3}$the Yangtze Economic Belt.

Sometimes a similar strategy is adopted in English but a detailed explanation is necessary:

(14) 按照“四个全面”战略布局。

Act in accordance with the Four-Pronged Comprehensive Strategy.

Note:

The strategy is to make comprehensive moves to:

1) finish building a moderately prosperous society;

2) deepen reform;

3) advance the law-based governance of China;

4) strengthen Party self-conduct.

Shortened forms in Chinese may find expression in some other structures, which, too, have to be expanded into their explicitly narrated expressions. For instance:

(15) 开展个人投资者境外投资试点,适时启动"深港通"试点。

Pilot private overseas investment, and launch the Shenzhen-Hong Kong Stock Connect on a trial basis at an appropriate time.

Here, 深港通 involves the shortened names of 深圳 and 香港, which have to be transformed to their respective full names. *Shenzhen-Hong Kong Stock Connect* is the understandable expression to English speakers. Similarly, 湘黔铁路 must be stated as *Hunan-Guizhou Railway Line* to facilitate understanding.

1.4 Sample

President Obama's 2016 State of the Union Address

Mr. Speaker, Mr. Vice President, Members of Congress, my fellow Americans:

议长先生、副总统先生、各位国会议员和美国同胞们:

Tonight marks the eighth year I've come here to report on the State of the Union. And for this final one, I'm going to try to make it shorter. I know some of you are antsy to get back to Iowa.

今晚是我在这里做国情咨文的第八个年头,也是最后一次。我将尽量简而言之。我知道你们中有些人急着回爱荷华州。

I also understand that because it's an election season, expectations for what we'll achieve this year are low. Still, Mr. Speaker, I appreciate the constructive approach you and the other leaders took at the end of last year to pass a budget and make tax cuts permanent for working families.

我也理解此时正当大选之季,因此公众对我们今年成就的期望并不高。但是,议长先生,您以及其他领导人去年年末通过了建设性的预算决议,使得工薪家庭减税计划能够长久实施下去,我对此深表感激。

So I hope we can work together this year on bipartisan priorities like criminal justice reform, and helping people who are battling prescription drug abuse. We just might surprise the cynics again.

因此我衷心希望今年两党能够在一些重要事务上同心协作,比如,推行刑事司法改革,帮助那些与处方药滥用行为抗争的人们。我们很可能会让质疑者们再次大吃一惊。

But tonight, I want to go easy on the traditional list of proposals for the year ahead. Don't worry, I've got plenty, from helping students learn to write computer code to personalizing medical treatments for patients. And I'll keep pushing for progress on the work that still needs doing.

但在今晚，我打算少谈些像往年那样的发展计划。别担心，我还是有很多计划要谈，比如，帮助学生学习编写计算机代码，以及对病人进行个性化治疗。我将继续推动这些未竟事业的进步。

Fixing a broken immigration system. Protecting our kids from gun violence. Equal pay for equal work, paid leave, raising the minimum wage. All these things still matter to hardworking families; they are still the right thing to do; and I will not let up until they get done.

完善有漏洞的移民体系。保护我们的孩子们免遭枪械暴力。继续推行同工同酬及带薪休假，并提高最低工资水平。所有的这一切对于努力工作的家庭来说依然至关重要；这些仍是我们要做的对的事情。我绝不会放松这些工作，直至他们完成为止。

But for my final address to this chamber, I don't want to talk just about the next year. I want to focus on the next five years, ten years, and beyond.

但这是我最后一次在此发表讲话，我不想只谈论来年的事宜。我想关注今后的五年、十年，甚至更久远的事情。

I want to focus on our future.

我更关注我们的未来。

We live in a time of extraordinary change — change that's reshaping the way we live, the way we work, our planet and our place in the world. It's change that promises amazing medical breakthroughs, but also economic disruptions that strain working families.

我们生活在一个充满巨变的时代，这场巨变改变了我们的生活、工作方式，改变了我们的星球和我们在世界上的地位。这种巨变预示着医学将出现重大突破，也会带来困扰着工薪家庭的经济动荡。

It promises education for girls in the most remote villages, but also connects terrorists plotting an ocean away. It's change that can broaden opportunity, or widen inequality. And whether we like it or not, the pace of this change will only accelerate.

它为生活在边远山区的女孩们带去教育的希望，却也使远距重洋的恐怖分子得以串通一气策划阴谋。这场巨变能够带来机遇，也会扩大不公。无论我们喜欢与否，这场巨变的进度只会越来越快。

America has been through big changes before — wars and depression, the influx of immigrants, workers fighting for a fair deal, and movements to expand civil rights. Each time, there have been those who told us to fear the future; who claimed we could slam the brakes on change, promising to restore past glory if we just got some group or idea that was threatening America under control.

美国曾经历过种种巨变——战争，萧条，移民涌入，工人运动，以及民权运动。每一次，总有人告诉我们要畏惧未来。每当美国受到某些组织或者言论威胁，将要失控，这些人就告诉我们要停止变革，并承诺恢复往日的辉煌。

And each time, we overcame those fears. We did not, in the words of Lincoln, adhere to the "dogmas of the quiet past." Instead we thought anew, and acted anew. We made change work for us, always extending America's promise outward, to the next frontier, to more and more people. And because we did — because we saw opportunity where others saw only peril — we emerged stronger and better than before.

但每一次，我们都能够克服恐惧。用林肯的话来说，我们并未遵循"平静的过去时代的信条"。相反地，我们能够用新的思维思考，以新的方式行事。我们巧妙地利用变化，始终将美国的潜力扩展至更广阔的前沿，惠及更多的民众。正缘于此——因为他人眼中的风险在我们看来是机遇——我们变得比以前更强更好。

What was true then can be true now. Our unique strengths as a nation — our optimism and work ethic, our spirit of discovery and innovation, our diversity and commitment to the rule of law — these things give us everything we need to ensure prosperity and security for generations to come.

过去的真理，现在亦未曾改变。我们的乐观主义与职业道德，我们的发现与创新精神，我们种族多样化和法治信条，这些都是我们作为一个国家所拥有的独一无二的优点，使我们具备了世代繁荣昌盛、国泰民安的一切条件。

In fact, it's that spirit that made the progress of these past seven years possible. It's how we recovered from the worst economic crisis in generations. It's how we reformed our health care system, and reinvented our energy sector; how we delivered more care and benefits to our troops and veterans, and how we secured the freedom in every state to marry the person we love.

事实上，正因有了这种精神力量，我们过去七年才可能取得进步。它使我们得以从几代以来最严重的经济危机中恢复；是我们改革医疗体系、改造能源部门的动力；保证了我们给予军人和老兵更多关心和福利。也正因为此，我们能够让每个州的人都获得了与所爱的人结婚的自由。

But such progress is not inevitable. It is the result of choices we make together. And we face such choices right now. Will we respond to the changes of our time with fear, turning inward as a nation, and turning against each other as a people? Or will we face the future with confidence in who we are, what we stand for, and the incredible things we can do together?

但是,这些进步并不是注定会发生的,而是我们共同选择的结果。我们当下正面临着这样的选择。面对时代的变化,我们是将以恐惧对之,闭门造车,各自为战?还是自我肯定,坚持立场,相信我们能共创奇迹?

So let's talk about the future, and four big questions that we as a country have to answer — regardless of who the next President is, or who controls the next Congress.

让我们先来谈谈未来,以及美国需要回答的四个大问题——无论下一届美国总统是谁,无论哪个党派掌控国会。

First, how do we give everyone a fair shot at opportunity and security in this new economy?

首先,我们如何在新经济中给每个人公平的机会和保障?

Second, how do we make technology work for us, and not against us — especially when it comes to solving urgent challenges like climate change?

第二,我们如何让技术为我们服务,而不是与我们对抗——尤其是面临气候变化这样急需应对的挑战的时候?

Third, how do we keep America safe and lead the world without becoming its policeman?

第三,我们如何保障美国的安全,同时,在不充当世界警察的前提下,引领整个世界?

And finally, how can we make our politics reflect what's best in us, and not what's worst?

最后,我们如何制定政策,使其反映出美国的好,而不是美国的恶?

Let me start with the economy, and a basic fact: the United States of America, right now, has the strongest, most durable economy in the world. We're in the middle of the longest streak of private-sector job creation in history.

我先说说经济,基本的事实是这样的:现在,在全球范围内,美国经济是最为强大且坚固的。纵观历史,我们现在处于私营部门连续创造就业机会最长的一段时期中。

More than 14 million new jobs; the strongest two years of job growth since the '90s; an unemployment rate cut in half. Our auto industry just had its best year ever.

Manufacturing has created nearly 900,000 new jobs in the past six years. And we've done all this while cutting our deficits by almost three-quarters.

我们创造了逾1400万个新的就业岗位;这是自20世纪90年代以来就业增长最为强劲的两年;失业率下降了一半。汽车行业也创造了最辉煌的一年。在过去的六年里,制造业创造了将近90万个新的就业岗位。而且,我们在取得这些成绩的同时,还将赤字减少了近四分之三。

Anyone claiming that America's economy is in decline is peddling fiction. What is true — and the reason that a lot of Americans feel anxious — is that the economy has been changing in profound ways, changes that started long before the Great Recession hit and haven't let up.

任何声称美国经济正在衰落的说法都是在传播虚构事实。实际情况——同时也是许多美国人感到焦虑的原因——是美国经济正在经历巨大变革,而且这变革早在大萧条发生之前就已经开始,到现在还没有结束。

Today, technology doesn't just replace jobs on the assembly line, but any job where work can be automated. Companies in a global economy can locate anywhere, and face tougher competition. As a result, workers have less leverage for a raise. Companies have less loyalty to their communities. And more and more wealth and income is concentrated at the very top.

今天,能够被高科技取代的工作岗位并不仅限于生产线,还包括任何可以实现自动化的岗位。在经济全球化中,公司可以落户于世界任何地方,也会面临更加激烈的竞争。其结果是,雇员要求加薪的筹码变少。公司对其所在群体的忠诚度更低。同时,越来越多的财富和收入积聚到社会顶层阶级手中。

All these trends have squeezed workers, even when they have jobs; even when the economy is growing. It's made it harder for a hardworking family to pull itself out of poverty, harder for young people to start on their careers, and tougher for workers to retire when they want to.

这些变化趋势挤压了雇员的生存空间,即使他们拥有工作,即使美国经济一直在增长。工薪家庭想要通过努力工作,摆脱贫困,年轻人想要开创自己的事业,雇员想要适时退休,都已经不太容易。

And although none of these trends are unique to America, they do offend our uniquely American belief that everybody who works hard should get a fair shot.

虽然面临这些变革的不只有美国,但是这些的确违背了独有的美国式信念,那就是,任何努力工作的人都应当得到公平待遇。

For the past seven years, our goal has been a growing economy that works better for everybody. We've made progress. But we need to make more. And despite all the political arguments we've had these past few years, there are some areas where Americans broadly agree.

在过去的七年中，我们的目标一直都是，保持经济增长，以造福每一个人。我们已经取得了一些进步。但是，我们需要继续努力。尽管在过去的一些年中，我们有过许多政治上的争论，但是在一些领域，我们取得了普遍的共识。

We agree that real opportunity requires every American to get the education and training they need to land a good-paying job. The bipartisan reform of No Child Left Behind was an important start, and together, we've increased early childhood education, lifted high school graduation rates to new highs, and boosted graduates in fields like engineering.

我们一致认为，真正的机会在于每一个美国人都能获得必要的教育及培训，让他们能够胜任一份收入理想的工作。"不让一个孩子掉队"的两党改革政策，就是一个重要的开端，同时，我们加强了儿童早期教育，进一步提高了高中毕业率，使工程学等专业毕业生得以增长。

In the coming years, we should build on that progress, by providing Pre-K for all, offering every student the hands-on computer science and math classes that make them job-ready on day one, and we should recruit and support more great teachers for our kids.

未来，我们要以这些成绩为基础，通过普及全民早教，让所有学生都接受计算机实践和数学课程培训，为他们将来步入职场做好准备。同时，我们要为孩子们招录更多优秀的教师，并给予这些教师更好的待遇。

And we have to make college affordable for every American. Because no hardworking student should be stuck in the red. We've already reduced student loan payments to ten percent of a borrower's income.

同时，我们要让每个美国人都能上得起大学。因为，勤奋的学生不应该因为贫困被挡在校门之外。我们已经将助学贷款的还款额降至借款人收入的10%。

Now, we've actually got to cut the cost of college. Providing two years of community college at no cost for every responsible student is one of the best ways to do that, and I'm going to keep fighting to get that started this year.

接下来，我们需要降低大学费用。两年制的社区大学将为每一位有责任感的学生提供免费教育，这是降低大学费用最理想的方式之一。我会不断努力让这个方案在今年启动。

Of course, a great education isn't all we need in this new economy. We also need benefits and protections that provide a basic measure of security. After all, it's not much of a stretch to say that some of the only people in America who are going to work the same job, in the same place, with a health and retirement package, for 30 years, are sitting in this chamber.

当然，在新经济中，我们所需要的不仅仅是优质的教育。我们还需要能够提供基本生活保障的福利和保护措施。如果说在座的各位，是美国为数不多的能够在同一个地方从事同一份工作 30 年，还能获得健康和养老保障的人，也不算夸张。

For everyone else, especially folks in their forties and fifties, saving for retirement or bouncing back from job loss has gotten a lot tougher. Americans understand that at some point in their careers, they may have to retool and retrain. But they shouldn't lose what they've already worked so hard to build.

而对于其他人，特别是四五十岁的美国人来说，为退休后的生存点钱或是在失业后重振旗鼓，已经越来越困难。大家都认识到，在他们职业生涯的某个时刻，他们不得不重新接受培训，重新学习技能。但是，他们不应当失去他们这么多年辛勤工作所获得的东西。

That's why Social Security and Medicare are more important than ever; we shouldn't weaken them, we should strengthen them. And for Americans short of retirement, basic benefits should be just as mobile as everything else is today.

这也是社会保障及医疗保险制度在今天尤为重要的原因；它们不该被弱化，而应进一步加强。对于退休年龄较晚的美国人，基本福利应与当今的其他事物一样尽可能移动化。

That's what the Affordable Care Act is all about. It's about filling the gaps in employer-based care so that when we lose a job, or go back to school, or start that new business, we'll still have coverage. Nearly eighteen million have gained coverage so far. Health care inflation has slowed. And our businesses have created jobs every single month since it became law.

这就是《平价医疗法案》的意义所在，这个法案旨在填补基于雇主的医疗保险系统的空缺，我们失业、返校求学或创业时，依然能享受医疗保障。目前为止，已有近 1800 万人受益。医疗费用通胀也有所缓解。自法案实施起，我们的企业每个月都能创造新的工作岗位。

Now, I'm guessing we won't agree on health care anytime soon. But there should be other ways both parties can improve economic security. Say a hardworking American loses his job — we shouldn't just make sure he can get unemployment insurance; we should make sure that program encourages him to retrain for a business that's ready to hire him.

我想我们在短期内还无法就医疗保险制度达成共识。但两党可以在改进经济保障制度的问题上采取一些新的措施。假设一位辛勤工作的美国人丢了工作，我们不该仅仅确保他能获得失业保险，而应确保这个制度能够支持他接受再培训以胜任新的工作。

If that new job doesn't pay as much, there should be a system of wage insurance in place so that he can still pay his bills. And even if he's going from job to job, he should still be able to save for retirement and take his savings with him. That's the way we make the new economy work better for everyone.

如果这份新工作的报酬不如上一份工作,那么就该有薪酬保障制度保证他能养活自己。即使他一直在换工作,也还能为退休储蓄并能支配自己的积蓄。这就是我们让大家更好地受益于新经济的方式。

I also know Speaker Ryan has talked about his interest in tackling poverty. America is about giving everybody willing to work a hand up, and I'd welcome a serious discussion about strategies we can all support, like expanding tax cuts for low-income workers without kids.

我知道国会众议院发言人保罗·瑞恩提到过他对解决贫困问题的看法。美国是一个会给每个愿意工作的人机会的国家,我欢迎大家提出可行性战略,如为无子女低收入人群减税的方案。

But there are other areas where it's been more difficult to find agreement over the last seven years — namely what role the government should play in making sure the system's not rigged in favor of the wealthiest and biggest corporations. And here, the American people have a choice to make.

但在过去七年里还有其他难以达成一致的领域,比如,政府应该扮演怎样的角色,才能保证制度不向最富有的财团和大公司倾斜。在此,美国人民需要做出选择。

I believe a thriving private sector is the lifeblood of our economy. I think there are outdated regulations that need to be changed, and there's red tape that needs to be cut. But after years of record corporate profits, working families won't get more opportunity or bigger paychecks by letting big banks or big oil or hedge funds make their own rules at the expense of everyone else; or by allowing attacks on collective bargaining to go unanswered.

蓬勃发展的私营经济是我们国家经济的命脉。我认为,其有些过时的规则需要改变,有些繁文缛节需要摒弃。在企业连续多年利润破纪录之后,如果让大银行、石油巨头或对冲基金制定只对自己有利的规则,或者允许对集体谈判的攻击置之不理,工薪阶层就无法获得更多机会和更多薪水。

Food Stamp recipients didn't cause the financial crisis; recklessness on Wall Street did. Immigrants aren't the reason wages haven't gone up enough; those decisions are made in the boardrooms that too often put quarterly earnings over long-term returns.

引发经济危机的不是那些领食物券的人,而是华尔街那些鲁莽行事的人。移民人口不是阻碍薪酬上涨的原因;那些决议是由董事会的人提出的,他们经常将季度分红看得比长期回报还重。

It's sure not the average family watching tonight that avoids paying taxes through offshore accounts. In this new economy, workers and start-ups and small businesses need more of a voice, not less. The rules should work for them.

可以肯定的是，正在看我演讲的普通家庭不会通过离岸账户避税。在新经济的形势下，工人、新兴企业和小型企业需要更多发言权。规则应该使他们受益。

And this year I plan to lift up the many businesses who've figured out that doing right by their workers ends up being good for their shareholders, their customers, and their communities, so that we can spread those best practices across America.

今年，我计划激励那些善待工人的企业，这些企业明白只有善待工人才能让股东、顾客和所在群体最终受益，这样我们才能在全美推行这种良策。

In fact, many of our best corporate citizens are also our most creative. This brings me to the second big question we have to answer as a country: how do we reignite that spirit of innovation to meet our biggest challenges?

事实上，我们有许多优秀的企业公民都是极富创造力的。这也是美国要回答的第二个大问题：如何重燃创新精神，迎接重大挑战？

Sixty years ago, when the Russians beat us into space, we didn't deny Sputnik was up there. We didn't argue about the science, or shrink our research and development budget. We built a space program almost overnight, and twelve years later, we were walking on the moon.

六十年前，俄罗斯人发射人造卫星，在太空领域领先于我们，这点我们并未否认。我们没有就科学水平进行争论，或缩减我们的研发预算。我们在很短的时间内制定了太空计划，十二年后，我们已经能在月球上行走。

That spirit of discovery is in our DNA. We're Thomas Edison and the Wright Brothers and George Washington Carver. We're Grace Hopper and Katherine Johnson and Sally Ride. We're every immigrant and entrepreneur from Boston to Austin to Silicon Valley racing to shape a better world. And over the past seven years, we've nurtured that spirit.

探索精神存在于我们的基因里。我们是托马斯·爱迪生、怀特兄弟、乔治·华盛顿·卡弗。我们是葛丽丝·霍普、凯瑟琳·约翰逊、莎莉·莱德。我们是从波士顿到奥斯丁再到硅谷的移民和企业家，我们力求建设更美好的世界。过去七年里，我们一直在培养这种精神。

We've protected an open internet, and taken bold new steps to get more students and low-income Americans online. We've launched next-generation manufacturing hubs, and online tools that give an entrepreneur everything he or she needs to start a business in a single day.

我们保护了开放的互联网,我们迈出了大胆的一大步,让更多学生和低收入者加入互联网这个大家庭。我们已经开始建设新一代制造业中心,我们的网络工具让企业家在一天内就能获得创立一个企业所需的一切。

But we can do so much more. Last year, Vice President Biden said that with a new moonshot, America can cure cancer. Last month, he worked with this Congress to give scientists at the National Institutes of Health the strongest resources they've had in over a decade. Tonight, I'm announcing a new national effort to get it done.

但是,我们能做的还不止这些。去年,副总统拜登曾说,要把治愈癌症作为一项新的登月计划去实现。上个月,他与国会通力合作,为国立卫生研究院的科学家们提供了大量资源,这是十多年来科学家们获得的最强有力的资源支持。今晚我宣布,我们将举全国之力促成这项新计划。

And because he's gone to the mat for all of us, on so many issues over the past forty years, I'm putting Joe in charge of Mission Control. For the loved ones we've all lost, for the family we can still save, let's make America the country that cures cancer once and for all.

在过去的四十年里,乔为我们在众多问题上竭尽心力,因此,我任命他主管这一抗癌计划。为了我们已逝去的亲人,为了我们还能拯救的家庭,我们应该携手,让美国成为一个彻底攻克癌症的国家。

1.5 A Glossary of Political System in Chinese and English

爱岗敬业 love one's work and be devoted to it
爱国民主党派 patriotic democratic parties
爱国守法 patriotism and observance of law
爱国统一战线 patriotic united front
爱国卫生运动 patriotic health and sanitation campaign
爱国主义教育基地 site for patriotic education/site rich in patriotic significance
安定的国内环境 stable domestic environment
安定团结的政治局面 political stability and unity
安分守己 abide by the law and behave oneself
安全责任制 safety responsibility system
按劳分配的原则 principle of distribution to each according to his work
按照国际惯例 act in accordance with international practices

按照客观规律和科学规律办事 act in compliance with objective and scientific laws

按照客观经济规律办事 act in accordance with objective economic laws

保持共产党员先进性 keep CPC members progressive, innovative and forward-thinking

诚实守信 be honest and keep one's word

城市低保对象 urban residents entitled to basic living allowances

创新型国家 innovation-oriented country

公共文化基础设施 culture-related facilities for public use

鼓励、支持和引导非公有制经济 encourage, support and guide the growth of the non-public sector of the economy

国家统一的职务与级别相结合的工资制度和工资正常增长机制 a unified national salary system based on position and rank and a mechanism for regular pay increases

完善城市低保制度 improve the system of urban subsistence allowances

完善国有资产监管体制,健全国有资本经营预算制度、经营业绩考核体系和国有资产重大损失责任追究制度 strengthen the oversight system for state assets by establishing a sound operating and budget system for state capital, a sound performance evaluation system and a sound system for assigning responsibility for major losses of state assets

完善境外投资协调机制和风险控制机制 improve the mechanisms for coordinating overseas investment and risk management

西部地区"两基"攻坚计划 the plan to make nine-year compulsory education universal and to eliminate illiteracy among the young and middle-aged in the western region

Chapter 2 Contrast of Sino-Western Cultures and Chinese-English Translation Texts in the Field of Law

2.1 What Is Law

Law is a system of rules that are enforced through social institutions to govern behavior. Laws can be made by a collective legislature or by a single legislator, resulting in statutes, by the executive through decrees and regulations, or by judges through binding precedent, normally in common law jurisdictions. Private individuals can create legally binding contracts, including arbitration agreements that may elect to accept alternative arbitration to the normal court process.

The formation of laws may be influenced by a constitution, written or tacit, and the rights encoded therein. The law shapes politics, economics, history and society in various ways and serves as a mediator of relations between people.

2.2 Cultural Contrast of Law in China and the West

2.2.1 Law in China

The two major Chinese philosophical schools, Confucianism(儒家) and Legalism (法家), strongly influenced the idea of law in China. Briefly, under Confucianism, the state should lead the people with virtue and thus create a sense of shame which will prevent bad conduct. Under Legalism, law is to be publicly promulgated standards of conduct backed by state coercion.

The tension between these two systems is that Confucianism relies on tradition to make the leader the head of household of all China, while Legalism makes standard law that even the emperor should be bound by. The common factor is that both endorse to different degrees a paternalistic conception of the state, which knows better than its citizens and makes laws to protect them. This concept persisted throughout the imperial period, into the republican period, and can still be seen acting today.

Unlike many other major civilizations where written law was held in honor and often attributed to divine origin, law in early China was viewed in purely secular terms, and its initial appearance was greeted with hostility by Confucian thinkers as indicative of a serious moral decline, a violation of human morality, and even a disturbance of the total cosmic order. Historically, people's awareness and acceptance of ethical norms was shaped far more by the pervasive influence of custom and usage of property and by inculcating moral precepts than by any formally enacted system of law. Early emperors, however, embraced the Legalist ideal as a way of exerting control over their large and growing territory and population. This process was integrated with traditional Chinese beliefs in the cosmic order, holding that correct behavior was behavior consonant with the appropriate responses set by fǎ(法). Xíng states the potential costs to the individual of exceeding them and imposes penalties for these actions.

The current constitution, created in 1982, states in Article V that no organization or individual is above the law and in Article III makes the People's Congresses and state administration responsible to the people, paving the way for later efforts to allow enforcement of individual rights. Passage of the Administrative Litigation Law of 1987 created legal recourse for individuals from arbitrary government action, an avenue previously unavailable. Despite the deep-seated norm against legal proceedings, litigation in the Chinese courts has increased dramatically, especially in recent years. The continuing weakness of courts resulting from their dependence on the local government for financial support and enforcement undermines the effectiveness of these remedies but this has also begun to change with China's initiatives to increase legal training and the professionalism of the judiciary.

2.2.2 Law in the West

The United Kingdom has three legal systems. English law, which applies in England and Wales, and Northern Ireland law, which applies in Northern Ireland, are based on common-law principles. Scots law, which applies in Scotland, is a pluralistic system based on civil-law principles, with common law elements dating back to the High Middle Ages.

The Supreme Court of the United Kingdom is the highest court in the land for all criminal and civil cases in England and Wales and Northern Ireland, and for all civil cases in Scots law. The Supreme Court came into being in October 2009, replacing the Appellate Committee of the House of Lords.

In England and Wales, the court system is headed by the Senior Courts of England and Wales, consisting of the Court of Appeal, the High Court of Justice (for civil cases) and the Crown Court (for criminal cases). The Courts of Northern Ireland follow the same pattern. In Scotland the chief courts are the Court of Session, for civil cases, and the High Court of Justiciary, for criminal cases. Sheriff courts have no equivalent outside Scotland, as they deal with both criminal and civil caseloads.

The United States legal system is the full interconnected system of judicial, regulatory and governmental authorities who together administer and enforce the laws of the United States, operate the judicial system, and resolve judicial disputes and appeals. It consists of various official bodies at the federal, state and local levels.

Federal courts address any legal issues covered by the statutes of the United States Code. They also hear any case falling under the jurisdiction of federal agencies.

The federal court system is made up of several levels of hierarchical court. The top-level court is the United States Supreme Court. Below this is the District Court of Appeals, and further below this is the United States District Courts, for various geographical areas as defined by the United States Congress.

State courts take a wide variety of forms, as defined by each state's legislature. For example, in New York, there is a Supreme Court which is actually the lowest-level trial court; its name is based on the fact that it is higher ranked than all administrative and local courts. The highest court in New York is the New York Court of Appeals.

2.3 Chinese-English Translation Texts in the Field of Law

2.3.1 English Favoring the Passive Voice, Chinese the Active

English has a strong inclination for the passive voice, especially in the style of legal discourses. That is to say, Chinese active voice statements often correspond to English passive ones. Besides, passive voice carries a more or less negative or unwanted connotation. It is the fact that, in Chinese, a positive statement is preferably made by the use of an active voice to show the narrator's direct mental access to the act or more eagerness to make it known to the addressee while negative statements are made in a more roundabout way to indicate the narrator's reluctance to declare it or to try to alienate the subject from the unwanted news by the use of a passive marker 被 or some alternative characters. Here are some examples to show the lack of voice correspondence in both languages:

(1) 借款方不按合同规定的用途使用借款，贷款方<u>有权</u>提前收回全部贷款，对违约使用的部分，收取每年12%的利息。

If the Borrower appropriates the loan from use stipulated herein, the Lender <u>is entitled to</u> immediately get back the entire loan and to claim for interests on the amount of loan appropriated at the rate of 12% per year.

In (1), active voice is used in the Chinese version but in English passive voice is the better choice. Similarly, in (2) the same principle is retained.

(2) 在不损害业主和/或PDP可能拥有的任何其它权利的前提下，应在下列情况下<u>征收</u>投标保证金。

Without prejudice to any other rights which the Owner and /or the PDP may possess, the Tender Bond shall be called upon under the following circumstances.

More examples in everyday talks:

(3) 常常六点半开灯。

The lights are usually turned on at 6:30.

(4) 正在安装一台新的发电机组。

A new generating set is being installed.

(5) 为什么总把麻烦推给我呢?

Why should the trouble be always put to me?

When it is hard to find an appropriate subject to realize the active voice structure in translation from English into Chinese, expressions with indefinite references such as 有人, 人们, 我们, 大家 or 人家 etc are the choice. For example:

(6) They were seen having a meeting.

有人看见他们正在开会。

(7) Electrons are known to be minute negative charges of electricity.

大家知道电子是极微小的负电荷。

(8) It is universally known that the world is made of matter.

人人都知道世界是由物质构成的。

2.3.2 English Favoring Lengthy Sentences, Chinese Short Ones

English uses lengthy sentences with coordinate or subordinate clauses adjoined together to embody a strong logical connection between the narrating chunks. This is done when a lot of cohesive devices, lexical or logical, are used. This is known to be hypotaxis (形合), where connecting links are abundantly used to define a logical integrity and hence achieve a lengthy statement.

As a contrast, Chinese prefers to use more clauses broken apart by the use of commas. The clauses can take care of their own logical connections through unstated semantic coherence. This is known to be parataxis (意合).

In this way English discourses are often compared to a big tree with branches and twigs spreading out in all directions, or a grape vine which covers a big acreage but actually it is but one plant. Chines discourses are known to be like bamboos, pointing straight up to the sky, with very few branches.

This being the contrast, changes have to be made in translating from Chinese into English or the other way around.

(9) $_1$If any services, mains, pipes and cable exist within the Site which may affect the Works,// $_2$the successful Tenderer shall liaise with the relevant utility authorities

or providers for provision of temporary works or permanent relocation of utilities to ensure that the utility services are not interrupted during the course of the Works and such costs are deemed to be included in the Contract Sum.

1如果场地内存在任何可能影响工程实施的设施、干线、管道和电缆，// 2中标者应联络相关的公共设施部门或供应商，// 3请求其对工程或公共设施进行临时或永久性迁移，//4 以确保公用设施在施工进程中不会中断，// 5且由此而产生的所有费用包含在合同金额中。

In (9) the English source language uses two clauses with each posing a structurally complex stretching, but its Chinese counterpart is composed of 5 shorter clauses. Readers may count them for testing.

Some more examples:

(10) 1When Zhou Enlai's door opened //2 they saw a slender man of more than average height with gleaming eyes and a face so striking that it bordered on the beautiful.

1周恩来的房门开了。//2 他们看到一个身材修长的人，//3 比普通人略高，//4 目光炯炯，//5 面貌引人注目，//6 称得上清秀。

The lengthy statement in Enlgish is eligible due to the use of conjunctions such as *when*, *of* , *with*, *and*, *so... that*. These connectors constitute the features of hypotaxis which are removed in the Chinese version. In their place commas are used to indicate a change of breath while semantic coherence is arrived at inherently.

Another example:

(11) 1I put on my clothes by the light of a half-moon just setting,// 2where rays streamed through the narrow window near my crib.

1半轮晓月渐渐西沉，//2 月光透过我小床旁边一个窄窄的窗子射进来。//3 我趁着月光穿上衣服。

The two clauses in English are broken down into three shorter ones with a change in order.

In Chinese we have been accustomed to some concise statements and have never felt the need of logical connectives, but in translating they have to be supplemented, e. g. :

(12) 上梁不正下梁歪。

If the upper beam is not straight, the lower ones will go aslant.

(13) 跑得了和尚，跑不了庙。

The monk may run away, but never his temple.

2.3.3 Nominalized Words in English Corresponding to Verbs in Chinese

Chinese and English differ substantially in many ways. In morphology, Chinese uses more verbs, many of which have to be nominalized in English, retaining part of their verbal features but giving way to the features of nouns in many ways. Consequently, the Chinese language is known to be dynamic, while the English language is statative, e. g. :

(14) After evaluation and acceptance of the Tenderer's submission, the Owner will then issue a Letter of Acceptance to the successful Tenderer.
对投标人提交的文件进行评估和验收之后，业主将向中标者发出中标通知书。

The underlined nominalizations in the source are verbs in the target, presenting a striking contrast in word form.

The causes there involved are multifold. One that comes to our mind first is that English words have derivative affixes switching from one word class to another. The Chinese language does not need the use of derivative affixes, one form poses varying functions in different context.

For example, 红 is known to be an adjective, but without any change in form it can be used as verb in 红起来了 or 红得发紫, and as noun in 这种红没有那种红那么亮. Similarly, 出版 keeps its orthographical identity when used in 老师出版了一本新书 or 这本书的出版是学术界的一件大事. In the former example 出版 is a verb but in the latter it is a noun or nominalization equivalent to *publication*.

Good translators or interpreters have to follow the rule here and take the initiative to undergo the shift of word forms: English nominalizations are often translated into Chinese verbs. Here are examples:

(15) The 1967 UN document calls for the settlement of the Middle East conflict on the basis of Israelis withdrawal from occupied territories and Arab acknowledgement of Israelis right to exist.
1967 年的联合国文件呼吁解决中东冲突，其基础是以色列从被占领的土地上撤退，阿拉伯国家则承认以色列人的生存权。

More examples might seem necessary:

(16) Starvation was a remote threat.
人们一时还不会饿死。

(17) The growing awareness by millions of people of their intolerable condition of life had prompted them to revote.
千百万人民日益意识到自己的生活条件不堪忍受，这促使他们起来反抗。

(18) He had entertained hopes of being admitted to a sight of the young ladies, of whose beauty he had heard much.
几位年轻小姐的美貌他耳闻已久，一直希望得以一睹芳容。

2.4 Sample

The sample cited here is an excerpt taken from Regulations of Jiangsu Province on

Labor Contracts(《江苏省劳动合同条例》).

第一章 总 则

Chapter Ⅰ General Provisions

第一条 为了完善劳动合同制度，明确劳动合同双方当事人的权利和义务，维护劳动者的合法权益，规范劳动用工管理，构建和发展和谐稳定的劳动关系，根据《中华人民共和国劳动法》《中华人民共和国劳动合同法》《中华人民共和国劳动合同法实施条例》等法律、行政法规，结合本省实际，制定本条例。

Article 1 These Regulations are enacted in accordance with the Labor Law of the People's Republic of China, the Labor Contract Law of the People's Republic of China and The Regulation on the Implementation of the Labor Contract Law of the People's Republic of China, and other relevant laws and administrative regulations, in light of the specific situation of this Province, and for the purposes of improving the labor contract regulations, specifying the rights and obligations of both parties to the labor contracts, safeguarding the legitimate rights and interests of the workers, standardizing the administration of labor use , and constructing and developing a harmonious and steady employment relationship.

第二条 本省行政区域内的企业、个体经济组织、民办非企业单位等组织(以下称用人单位)与劳动者建立劳动关系，订立、履行、变更、解除或者终止劳动合同，适用本条例。

Article 2 These Regulations shall apply to the establishment of employment relationship between enterprises, individual economic organizations, non-enterprise private entities and other entities (hereinafter referred to as the employers) and the workers thereof, as well as the conclusion, performance, alteration, discharge or termination of labor contracts there between.

依法成立的基金会和会计师事务所、律师事务所等组织，属于前款所称的用人单位。国家机关、事业单位、社会团体和与其建立劳动关系的劳动者，订立、履行、变更、解除或者终止劳动合同，依照本条例执行。

Organizations such as foundations, accountant firms and law firms founded according to laws shall be included into the employers referred to in the previous paragraph. These Regulations shall also apply to state organs, public institutions, social organizations and workers bound up by labor contracts concerning the conclusion, performance, alteration, discharge or termination of labor contracts.

第三条 劳动合同是劳动者与用人单位明确劳动关系双方权利和义务的协议。用人单位与劳动者建立劳动关系，应当订立书面劳动合同。

Article 3 The labor contract is the agreement reached by the worker and the employer to clarify the rights and duties of the two parties of employment relationship. Where an employer establishes employment relationship with a worker, a labor contract in a written form shall be concluded.

第四条 用人单位应当保障劳动者的人格尊严、安全健康和获取劳动报酬、参与民主管理等权利，不得通过制定规章制度免除用人单位责任、加重劳动者责任、排除劳动者合法权利。劳动者应当遵守用人单位依法制定的规章制度，按照劳动法律、法规的规定和集体合同、劳动合同的约定行使权利、履行义务，不得损害用人单位的合法权益。

Article 4 Employers shall ensure workers' dignity, safety and health and their rights to gain remuneration, participate in democratic management, etc., and shall not disclaim their legal liability, enhance the workers' obligation or deny workers' rights by formulating bylaws. Workers shall abide by the bylaws stipulated by the employer according to law, perform the rights and duties according to the provisions of labor contracts, and shall not impair the legal rights of employers.

用人单位依法制定、修改或者决定的直接涉及劳动者切身利益的规章制度和重大事项，应当主动、如实告知劳动者，或者采取公告栏、书面文本、电子邮件、本单位网站等便于劳动者知晓的方式公示。

Where employers formulate, revise or decide the bylaws and important matters in direct relation to the vital interests of workers, they shall actively and authentically inform workers, or publicize them in such forms as bulletin boards, written texts, emails, the website of the unit, which are convenient for workers to know.

第五条 县级以上地方人民政府应当将维护和促进劳动关系和谐稳定作为重要职责，广泛听取用人单位、劳动者、工会组织和用人单位代表组织等相关方面的意见，研究制定涉及劳动关系的政策、措施。

Article 5 The local people's government at or above the county level shall regard maintaining and promoting harmonious and steady employment relationship as their major duties, widely solicit opinions from employers, workers or the labor union and relevant delegate organization of employers, research and formulate policies and measures related to employment relationship.

第六条 县级以上地方人民政府劳动行政部门负责对本行政区域内劳动合同制度的实施进行指导、协调、管理和监督检查，依法协调劳动关系，妥善处理劳动争议。基层劳动就业社会保障公共服务组织协助做好本辖区劳动合同制度实施的有关工作。

Article 6 The labor administrative department of the local people's government at or above the county level shall be responsible for guidance, coordination, administration, supervision and inspection of the implementation of the labor contract regulations within its administrative region, coordinate employment relationship according to law and properly deal with labor disputes. Public service organizations of employment and social security at the grass-roots level shall assist in relevant work on implementation of the labor contract regulations within its administrative region.

第七条　县级以上地方人民政府劳动行政部门会同工会和用人单位代表组织组成协调劳动关系委员会，协调处理劳动关系的重大问题。

Article 7　The labor administrative department of the local people's government at or above the county level shall set up a committee for coordinating labor relationship in collaboration with the labor union and delegate organizations of employers, and coordinate to deal with major issues in labor relationship.

第八条　工会依法维护劳动者的合法权益，对用人单位遵守劳动法律、法规制定劳动规章制度，履行劳动合同和集体合同等情况进行监督。

Article 8　The labor union shall safeguard workers' legitimate rights and interests in accordance with relevant laws and surveil the employer's performance on following labor laws and regulations, formulating labor bylaws, and carrying out labor contracts and collective contracts, etc.

第九条　共产主义青年团、妇女联合会、残疾人联合会以及其他社会组织应当促进平等就业工作，消除就业歧视，维护劳动者合法权益。

Article 9　The Communist Youth League, Women's Federation, Federation of the Disabled People and other social groups shall promote fair employment, discard employment discrimination, and safeguard employees' legal rights and interests.

第十条　县级以上地方人民政府应当对模范遵守劳动法律、法规，构建和谐劳动关系的用人单位和个人予以表彰。

Article 10　The local people's government at or above the county level shall reward the employers and individuals that abide by labor laws and regulations, and construct a harmonious labor relationship.

2.5 A Glossary of Law in English and Chinese

暴乱 riot

粗狂行为罪 indecent exposure

盗窃 burglary

盗窃 theft

赌博 gambling
反叛 mutiny
犯规/违反行为 violation
非重刑罪/轻罪 misdemeanor
诽谤 defamation
诽谤 slandering
过失杀人罪 manslaughter
贿赂 bribery
假账 false accounting
劫持 hijacking
恐吓 intimidation
勒索 blackmail
流氓行为 hooliganism
乱伦 incest
麻醉品交易 narcotics trafficking
冒充 personation
谋杀 murder
殴打 battery
欺诈 fraud
强奸 raping
抢劫 robbery
敲诈 extortion
侵犯 encroachment
侵吞、侵占 defalcation/embezzlement
杀婴罪 infanticide
擅闯 trespassing
失当行为 misfeasance
失职行为 delinquency
伪证 perjury
洗钱罪 money laundry
性骚扰 sex assault
性骚扰 sex-harassment
严重猥亵 gross indecency
阴谋罪 conspiracy
诈骗勒索 racketeering
种族灭绝 genocide

滋扰罪 affray
滋扰罪 nuisance
纵火罪 arson
走私 smuggling

Chapter 3 Contrast of Sino-Western Cultures and Chinese-English Translation Texts in the Field of Literature

3.1 What Is Literature

Literature, in its broadest sense, consists of any written productions. More restrictively, it refers to those deemed to have artistic or intellectual value, or which deploy language in ways that differ from ordinary usage.

Literature can be classified according to whether it is fiction or non-fiction and whether it is poetry or prose; it can be further distinguished according to major forms such as the novel, short story or drama; and works are often categorized according to historical periods or their adherence to certain aesthetic features or expectations.

Literature has changed its meaning over time: nowadays it can broaden to include non-written verbal art forms, and thus it is difficult to agree on its origin, which can be paired with that of language or writing itself.

3.2 Cultural Contrast of Literature in China and the West

3.2.1 Literature in China

Chinese literature extends thousands of years, from the earliest recorded dynastic court archives to the mature vernacular fiction novels that arose during the Ming Dynasty to entertain the masses of literate Chinese. The introduction of widespread woodblock printing during the Tang Dynasty (618—907) and the invention of movable type printing by Bi Sheng (990—1051) during the Song Dynasty (960—1279) rapidly spread written knowledge throughout China.

The rich tradition of Chinese poetry began with two influential collections.

In northern China, the *Shijing* or *Classic of Poetry* comprises over 300 poems in a variety of styles ranging from those with a strong suggestion of folk music to ceremonial hymns. The word *shi* (诗) has the basic meaning of poem or poetry, as well as its use in criticism to describe one of China's lyrical poetic genres. Its stately verses are usually composed of couplets with lines of four characters each (or four syllables, as Chinese characters are monosyllabic), and a formal structure of end rhymes. Many of these early poems establish the later tradition of starting with a description of nature that leads into emotionally expressive statements, known as *bi*, *xing*, or sometimes *bixing*.

In southern China, the *Chuci*(楚辞)is ascribed to Qu Yuan (340 BC—278 BC) and his follower Song Yu (fl. 3rd century BC) and is distinguished by its more emotionally intense affect, often full of despair and descriptions of the fantastic. In some of its sections, the *Chuci* uses a six-character per line meter, dividing these lines into couplets separated in the middle by a strong caesura, producing a driving and dramatic rhythm. Both the *Shijing* and the *Chuci* have remained influential throughout Chinese history.

During the greater part of China's first great period of unification, begun with the short-lived Qin Dynasty and followed by the centuries-long Han Dynasty, the shi form of poetry underwent little innovation. But a distinctively descriptive and erudite fu(赋) form (not the same fu character as that used for the bureau of music) developed that has been called "rhyme-prose," a uniquely Han offshoot of Chinese poetry's tradition.

Equally noteworthy is Music Bureau poetry (yuefu,乐府), collected and presumably refined popular lyrics from folk music. The end of the Han witnessed a resurgence of the shi poetry, with the anonymous 19 Old Poems. This collection reflects the emergence of a distinctive five-character line that later became shi poetry's most common line length. From the Jian'an reign period (196 AD—220 AD) onward, the five-character line became a focus for innovations in style and theme. The Cao family, rulers of the Wei Dynasty (220 AD—265 AD) during the post-Han Three Kingdoms period, distinguished themselves as poets by writing poems filled with sympathy for the day-to-day struggles of soldiery and the common people. Taoist philosophy became a different, common theme for other poets, and a genre emphasizing true feeling emerged led by Ruan Ji (210—263). The landscape genre of Chinese nature poetry emerged under the brush of Xie Lingyun (385—433), as he innovated distinctively descriptive and complementary couplets composed of five-character lines. A farmland genre was born in obscurity by Tao Qian(365—427), also known as Tao Yuanming, as he labored in his fields and then wrote extolling the influence of wine. Toward the close of this period in which many later-developed themes were first experimented with, the Xiao family of the Southern Liang Dynasty (502—557) engaged in highly refined and often denigrated court-style poetry lushly describing sensual delights as well as the description of objects.

Reunified China's Tang Dynasty (618—907) high culture set a high point for many things, including poetry. Various schools of Buddhism (a religion from India) flourished as represented by the Chan (or Zen) beliefs of Wang Wei (701—761). His quatrains (绝句) describing natural scenes are world-famous examples of excellence, each couplet conventionally containing about two distinct images or thoughts per line. Tang poetry's big star is Li Bai (701—762), also pronounced and written as Li Bo, who worked in all major styles, both the more free old style verse (古体诗) and the tonally regulated new style verse (近体诗). Regardless of genre, Tang poets notably strove to perfect a style in which poetic subjects are exposed and evident, often without directly referring to the emotional thrust at hand. The poet Du Fu (712—770) excelled at regulated verse and use of the seven-character line, writing denser poems with more allusions as he aged, experiencing hardship and writing about it. A parade of great Tang poets also includes Chen Zi'ang (661—702), Wang Zhihuan (688—742), Meng Haoran (689—740), Bai Juyi (772—846), Li He (790—816), Du Mu (803—852), Wen Tingyun (812—870), and Li Shangyin (813—858), (listed chronologically) whose poetry delights in allusions that often remain obscure, and whose emphasis on the seven-character line also contributed to the emerging posthumous fame of Du Fu, now ranked alongside Li Bai. The distinctively different ci poetry form began its development during the Tang as Central Asian and other musical influences flowed through its cosmopolitan society.

China's Song Dynasty (960—1279), another reunification era after a brief period of disunity, initiated a fresh high culture. Several of its greatest poets were capable government officials as well, including Ouyang Xiu (1007—1072), Su Shi (1037—1101), and Wang Anshi (1021—1086). The ci form flourished as a few hundred songs became standard templates for poems with distinctive and variously set meters. The free and expressive style of Song high culture has been contrasted with majestic Tang poems by centuries of subsequent critics who engage in fierce arguments over which dynasty had the best poetry. Additional musical influences contributed to the Yuan Dynasty's (1271—1368) distinctive qu opera culture and spawned the sanqu form of individual poems based on it.

Classical Chinese poetry composition became a conventional skill of the well-educated throughout the Ming (1368—1644) and Qing (1644—1911) dynasties. Over a million poems have been preserved, including those by women and by many other diverse voices. Painter-poets, such as Shen Zhou (1427—1509), Tang Yin (1470—1524), Wen Zhengming (1470—1559), and Yun Shouping (1633—1690), created worthy conspicuous poems as they combined art, poetry and calligraphy with brush on paper. Poetry composition competitions were socially common, as depicted in novels, for example over dessert after a nice dinner. The Song versus Tang debate continues through the centuries. While China's later imperial period does not seem to have broken new ground for innovative approaches to poetry, picking through its vast body of preserved works remains a scholarly challenge, so new treasures may yet be restored from obscurity.

After the 14th century, vernacular fiction became popular, at least outside of court circles. Vernacular fiction covered a broader range of subject matter and was longer and more loosely structured than literary fiction. One of the masterpieces of Chinese vernacular fiction is the 18th-century domestic novel *Dream of the Red Chamber*.

The literary scene in the first few years before the collapse of the Qing in 1911 was dominated by popular love stories, some written in the classical language and some in the vernacular. This entertainment fiction would later be labeled "Mandarin Ducks and Butterfly" fiction by New Culturalists, who despised its lack of social engagement. Throughout much of the Republican era, Butterfly fiction would reach many more readers than its "progressive" counterpart.

Chinese literature at the beginning of the 21st century shows signs of overcoming the commercialization of literature of the 1980s and 1990s. An example is Han Han's (韩寒) novel *His Land* (《他的国》, 2009), which is written in a social critical surrealistic style against the uncritical mainstream, but ranked 1st in 2009 Chinese bestseller list. Another example is Yan Ge's novel *Family of Joy* (《我们家》, 2013), which is written in Sichuan dialect and won the Chinese Media Group New Talent Award in 2013.

Guan Moye (管谟业, born 17 February 1955), better known by the pen name Mo Yan (莫言), is a Chinese novelist and short story writer. He is best known to Western readers for his 1987 novel *Red Sorghum Clan*, of which the *Red Sorghum* and *Sorghum Wine* volumes were later adapted for the film *Red Sorghum*. In 2012, Mo was awarded the Nobel Prize in Literature for his work as a writer "who with hallucinatory realism merges folk tales, history and the contemporary."

3.2.2 Literature in the West

English descends from the language spoken by the north Germanic tribes who settled in England from the 5th century A. D. onwards. They had no writing system until they learned the Latin alphabet from Roman missionaries. The earliest written works in Old English were probably composed orally at first, and may have been passed on from speaker to speaker before being written.

From 1066 onwards, the first great name in English literature is that of Geoffrey Chaucer (c. 1343—1400). Chaucer introduces the iambic pentameter line, the rhyming couplet and other rhymes used in Italian poetry. Some of Chaucer's work is prose and some is lyric poetry, but his greatest work is mostly narrative poetry, which we find in *Troilus and Criseyde* and *The Canterbury Tales*. Modern lyric poetry in English begins in the early 16th century with the work of Sir Thomas Wyatt (1503—1542) and Henry Howard, Earl of Surrey (1517—1547).

The first great English dramatist is Marlowe. The greatest of Elizabethan lyric poets is John Donne (1572—1631), whose short love poems are characterized by wit and irony, as he seeks to wrest meaning from experience. Jonathan Swift (1667—1745) wrote satires in verse and prose. He is best-known for the extended prose work *Gulliver's Travels*, in which a fantastic account of a series of travels is the vehicle for satirizing familiar English institutions, such as religion, politics and law. Another writer who uses prose fiction, this time much more naturalistic, to explore other questions of politics or economics is Daniel Defoe (1661—1731), author of *Robinson Crusoe* and *Moll Flanders*.

The first English novel is generally accepted to be *Pamela* (1740), by Samuel Richardson (1689—1761): this novel takes the form of a series of letters; Pamela, a virtuous housemaid resists the advances of her rich employer, who eventually marries her. Richardson's work was almost at once satirized by Henry Fielding (1707—1754) in *Joseph Andrews* (Joseph is depicted as the brother of Richardson's Pamela Andrews) and *Tom Jones*.

After Fielding, the novel is dominated by two great figures — Sir Walter Scott (1771—1832) and Jane Austen (1775—1817), who typify, respectively, the new regional, historical romanticism and the established, urbane classical views.

Romanticism is the revolt of the senses or passions against the intellect and of the individual against the consensus. Its first stirrings may be seen in the work of William Blake (1757—1827), and in continental writers such as the Swiss philosopher Jean-Jacques Rousseau and the German playwrights Johann Christoph Friedrich Schiller and Johann Wolfgang von Goethe.

The publication, in 1798, by the poets William Wordsworth (1770—1850) and Samuel Taylor Coleridge (1772—1834) of a volume entitled *Lyrical Ballads* is a significant event in English literary history.

John Keats (1795—1821) and his friend Percy Bysshe Shelley (1792—1822) are marked by an attempt to make language beautiful, and by an interest in remote history and exotic places. George Gordon, Lord Byron (1788—1824) uses romantic themes, sometimes comically, to explain contemporary events. Romanticism begins as a revolt against established views, but eventually becomes the established outlook. Wordsworth becomes a kind of national monument, while the Victorians make what was at first revolutionary seem familiar, domestic and sentimental.

Charles Dickens (1812—1870) is noted for the complexity of his best work, the variety of tone, the use of irony and caricature. *Great Expectations*, *Bleak House*, *Our Mutual Friend* and *Little Dorrit* are works with which every student should be acquainted.

Charlotte Brontë (1816—1855) and her sisters Emily (1818—1848) and Anne (1820—1849) are understandably linked together, but their work differs greatly.

William Butler Yeats (1865—1939) is one of two figures who dominate modern poetry, the other being Thomas Stearns Eliot (1888—1965). The work of these two has overshadowed the work of the best late Victorian, Edwardian and Georgian poets, some of whom came to prominence during the First World War.

The late Victorian and early modern periods are spanned by two novelists of foreign birth: the American Henry James (1843—1916) and the Pole Joseph Conrad (Josef Korzeniowski, 1857—1924). Other notable writers of the early part of the century include

George Bernard Shaw (1856—1950), H. G. Wells (1866—1946), and E. M. Forster (1879—1970). Masters of modern writing include James Joyce (1882—1941), Virginia Woolf (1882—1941), and D. H. Lawrence (1885—1930). Between the two wars, a revival of romanticism in poetry is associated with the work of W. H. (Wystan Hugh) Auden (1907—1973), Louis MacNeice (1907—1963) and Cecil Day-Lewis (1904—1972).

American literature is written or produced inside the borders of the United States and its preceding colonies. American literary tradition is linked to the broader tradition of English literature.

Nathaniel Hawthorne (1804—1864) is notable for his masterpiece, *The Scarlet Letter*, a novel about adultery. Hawthorne influenced Herman Melville (1819—1891) who is notable for the books *Moby-Dick* and *Billy Budd*. America's two greatest 19th-century poets were Walt Whitman (1819—1892) and Emily Dickinson (1830—1886). American poetry reached a peak in the early-to-mid-20th century, with such noted writers as Wallace Stevens, T. S. Eliot, Robert Frost, Ezra Pound, Hart Crane, and E. E. Cummings. Mark Twain (the pen name used by Samuel Langhorne Clemens, 1835—1910) was the first major American writer to be born away from the East Coast. Henry James (1843—1916) was notable for novels like *The Turn of the Screw*. At the beginning of the 20th century, American novelists included Edith Wharton (1862—1937), Stephen Crane (1871—1900), Theodore Dreiser (1871—1945), and Jack London (1876—1916). Experimentation in style and form is seen in the works of Gertrude Stein (1874—1946).

American writers expressed disillusionment following WWI. The stories and novels of F. Scott Fitzgerald (1896—1940) capture the mood of the 1920s, and John Dos Passos wrote about the war. Ernest Hemingway (1899—1961) became notable for *The Sun Also Rises* and *A Farewell to Arms*; in 1954, he won the Nobel Prize in Literature. William Faulkner (1897—1962) is notable for novels like *The Sound and the Fury*. American drama attained international status only in the 1920s and 1930s, with the works of Eugene O'Neill, who won four Pulitzer Prizes and the Nobel Prize. In the middle of the 20th century, American drama was dominated by the work of playwrights Tennessee Williams and Arthur Miller, as well as by the maturation of the American musical.

John Steinbeck (1902—1968), a Depression era writer, is notable for his novel *The Grapes of Wrath*. Henry Miller assumed a unique place in American Literature in the 1930s when his semi-autobiographical novels were banned from the US.

America's involvement in World War II influenced the creation of works such as Norman Mailer's *The Naked and the Dead* (1948), Joseph Heller's *Catch-22* (1961) and Kurt Vonnegut Jr.'s *Slaughterhouse-Five* (1969).

3.3 Chinese-English Translation Texts in the Field of Literature

3.3.1 Multilevel Correspondence in Lexicon, Rhetoric and Sentence Structure

Literature serves not only for getting through information, but to a greater extent for aesthetic purposes. So it is not risky to claim that literature is a school of aesthetics. To achieve this end, the translator or interpreter has to pay sufficient attention to the choice of word, the full display of rhetoric and the proper arrangement of sentence structure. (1) is a good example.

(1) Studies serve for delight, for ornament, and for ability.
读书之用有三，一为怡神旷心，二为增趣添雅，三为长才益智。

The source text is very brief and beautifully stated. The three prepositional phrases, which lie in juxtaposition, display the author's wit of brevity and being explicit. The translator has perceived this and properly utilized the Chinese aesthetic resources to verbalize the information and aesthetic value: four-character idioms in Chinese are fossilized language materials transmitted from the classic Chinese which carry the merits of being brief and formal in style. The three idioms 怡神旷心, 增趣添雅 and 长才益智 are rhythmical and serve for prosodic entertainment. They are good matches for the three prepositional phrases *for delight*, *for ornament*, and *for ability* in information and in aesthetic effects.

More examples can be found in the following examples. The four-character idioms are well chosen and echo the original text perfectly.

(2) Seek not proud riches but such as thou mayest bet justly, use soberly, distribute cheerfully and leave contentedly.
千万别为摆阔炫耀而追求财富，只挣你取之有道、用之有度、施之有乐且遗之有慰的钱财。

(3) Honor hath three things in it: the vantage ground to do good; the approach to kings and principal persons; and the raising of a man's own fortunes.
欲求高位者可怀有三种动机：一是想获得佐政济世的条件，二是想获得攀龙附凤的机会；三是想获得发财致富的时运。

The following example is well known for the premium choice of classic Chinese words for archaic English words. A fantastic match!

(4) Saith the Pythonissa to Saul, Tomorrow thou and Thy son shall be with me.
如女巫曾对扫罗说：明日汝及诸子将与吾同在。

Use of archaic words helps to render the discourse more solemn and ceremonious. The translator has the professional duty to ensure that the target language reader perceives and benefits from an approximating amount as the source language reader. Another example can be found in (5).

(5) It is a pleasure to stand upon the shore and to see ships tossed upon the sea; a pleasure to stand in the window of a castle, and to see a battle, and the adventures thereof below; but no pleasure is comparable to the standing upon the vantage ground of truth (a hill not to be commanded, and where the air is always dear and serene) and to see the errors, and wanderings, and mists, and tempests, in the vale below.

登高岸而濒水伫观舟揖颠簸于海上,不亦快哉;踞城堡而倚窗凭眺两军酣战于脚下,不亦快哉;然断无任何快事堪比凌真理之绝顶(一座巍然高耸且风清气朗的峰顶),一览深谷间的谬误与彷徨,迷雾与风暴。

The target text in (5) is more classical than contemporary, the repeated use of 不亦快哉 is most appropriate in conveying the source speaker's happy state of mind. The symmetrical structure adds the momentum perceivable in the source language.

3.3.2 Resorting to Phonetic Transcription in Chinese

Literature is rooted in a specific nation, depicting how the people belonging to a particular culture think, feel, live, and decease. Therefore literature is national. Of course we do not mean to deny that there is something transcending the human race and is universal. The culture-specific nature of literature will have to face the problem of word choice which is likewise culture-specific. Transliteration, which means zero translation or copying the phonological value of the word in the source language, is a good strategy to translate the culture-specific concepts which are vacant in the target language.

(6) 上官吕氏把簸箕里的尘土倒在揭了席、卷了草的土炕上……

Shangguan Lu emptied her dustpan onto the exposed surface of the kang, whose grass mat and bedding had been rolled up and put to one side.

Kang is used in northern China where the rural people build a stove with clay and upon it a bed is made, when smoldering fire is kept in the stove sufficient heat can go up to the bedding at the top to keep the sleepers warm in winter. *Kang* is culture-specific and does not expect to find an equivalent word in the English language, so transliteration is the best way out but of course explanation is necessary by the use of a footnote or in-text introduction.

In (7), *zhuangyuan* is transliterated with an attached explanation *top scholar at the Imperial Examination* to make it understandable to the target language readers.

(7) 我家漩儿,非嫁个状元不可的!

Our Xuan'er will marry a zhuangyuan, top scholar at the Imperial Examination.

3.3.3 Resorting to Paraphrasing in Chinese

Paraphrasing is an alternate strategy in translating culture-specific concepts. Its essence is to evade the seemingly untranslatable concept and take a roundabout path in explaining it to the readers of the target language. (8) is an example.

(8) 这是马童的爷爷，清朝时中过举人，文化水平很高。

It was Ma Tong's grandfather, a highly educated onetime official during the Qing dynasty.

The paraphrasing is successful because it pinpoints *juren*'s social position and its existing stage in history. Such information suffices for the readers of the English language.

Paraphrasing may resemble the tactics of literal translation: a word-for-word translation is valid for some allusions or historical stories or legends.

In (9) the cultural image of a humble toad expecting to eat the meat of a swan is literally expressed. Here orientation metaphors are inherent: UP IS GOOD is an implied radical metaphor, so is LOW IS BAD. Swans flying in the sky is considered a beautiful image which is transferred to its meat, toads crawling along the mud is thought to be humble. Of course, swans amusing human eyes while toads looking ugly is a contributing factor to the judgment of their values.

(9) "姓沙的，你癞蛤蟆想吃天鹅肉，做梦去吧!"

"You there, Sha," she said, "like the toad who wants to feast on a swan, you can just dream on!"

Similar strategies are applied in (10) and (11).

(10) 我们走运时，您没少跟着沾光。现在我们走背字，连我们的孩子也不吃香了是不是? 娘，一碗水要端平!

"Mother," Pandi said, "when the good days came around, you shared in our good fortune. Now that we've run into a spell of bad luck, not even our children are spared, is that it? A bowl has to be held straight so the water won't spill."

(11) 扬州城自古为"繁华胜地"。唐时杜牧有诗云:"十年一觉扬州梦，赢得青楼薄幸名"。古人云人生乐事，莫过于"腰缠十万贯，骑鹤上扬州"。

The city of Yangzhou has long been synonymous in China with wealth, pleasure, and sybaritic luxury. The great poet Du Mu, of the late Tang dynasty, sums it up in his famous lines: From my Yangzhou Dream I wake at last—Ten years a rake, ten years gone so fast! And as the old saying has it, one of life's greatest pleasures has always been to strap on a myriad strings of cash, and ride a crane to Yangzhou town.

In (11), the citations are literally translated or paraphrased and the result is obvious that English readers can understand them. One more point worth mentioning is that extra information is given to explain Du Mu, his identiy *the great poet* is made clear and the historical period he belonged to is added: *the late Tang dynasty*. Such information may be taken for granted to the Chinese readers but English readers will feel it imperative to get informed.

3.5 Samples

Three samples are chosen respectively from W. Shakespeare's *Hamlet* (exerpt), F. Bacon's *Of Studies*, and Su Shi's *The Midautumn Festival*.

1. W. Shakespeare's *Hamlet* (exerpt)

To be, or not to be: that is the question:
Whether 'tis nobler in the mind to suffer
The slings and arrows of outrageous fortune,
Or to take arms against a sea of troubles,
And by opposing end them?
生存还是毁灭,这是一个值得考虑的问题;
默然忍受命运的暴虐的毒箭,或是挺身反抗人世的无涯的苦难,
通过斗争把它们扫清,这两种行为,哪一种更高贵?

To die, to sleep;
No more; and by a sleep to say we end
The heart-ache and the thousand natural shocks
That flesh is heir to, 'tis a consummation
Devoutly to be wish'd.
死了;睡着了;什么都完了;
要是在这一种睡眠之中,我们心头的创痛,
以及其他无数血肉之躯所不能避免的打击,都可以从此消失,
那正是我们求之不得的结局。

To die, to sleep;
To sleep: perchance to dream: ay, there's the rub;
For in that sleep of death what dreams may come
When we have shuffled off this mortal coil,
Must give us pause: there's the respect
That makes calamity of so long life.
死了;睡着了;睡着了也许还会做梦;
嗯,阻碍就在这儿:
因为当我们摆脱了这一具朽腐的皮囊以后,
在那死的睡眠里,究竟将要做些什么梦,那不能不使我们踌躇顾虑。
人们甘心久困于患难之中,也就是为了这个缘故。

For who would bear the whips and scorns of time,
The oppressor's wrong, the proud man's contumely,
The pangs of despised love, the law's delay,
The insolence of office and the spurns
That patient merit of the unworthy takes,
When he himself might his quietus make
With a bare bodkin? who would fardels bear,
To grunt and sweat under a weary life,
But that the dread of something after death,
The undiscover'd country from whose bourn
No traveller returns, puzzles the will
And makes us rather bear those ills we have
Than fly to others that we know not of?
谁愿意忍受人世的鞭挞和讥嘲、压迫者的凌辱、
傲慢者的冷眼、被轻蔑的爱情的惨痛、法律的迁延、
官吏的横暴和费尽辛勤所换来的小人的鄙视，
要是他只要用一柄小小的刀子，就可以清算他自己的一生？
谁愿意负着这样的重担，
在烦劳的生命的压迫下呻吟流汗，倘不是因为惧怕不可知的死后，
惧怕那从来不曾有一个旅人回来过的神秘之国，
是它迷惑了我们的意志，使我们宁愿忍受目前的磨折，
不敢向我们所不知道的痛苦飞去？

Thus conscience does make cowards of us all;
And thus the native hue of resolution
Is sicklied o'er with the pale cast of thought,
And enterprises of great pith and moment
With this regard their currents turn awry,
And lose the name of action. —Soft you now!
The fair Ophelia! Nymph, in thy orisons
Be all my sins remember'd.
这样，重重的顾虑使我们全变成了懦夫，
决心的赤热的光彩，被审慎的思维盖上了一层灰色，
伟大的事业在这一种考虑之下，也会逆流而退，
失去了行动的意义。

2. F. Bacon's *Of Studies*

Studies serve for delight, for ornament, and for ability. Their chief use for delight, is in privateness and retiring; for ornament, is in discourse; and for ability, is in the judgment and disposition of business.

读书足以怡情,足以傅彩,足以长才。其怡情也,最见于独处幽居之时;其傅彩也,最见于高谈阔论之中;其长才也,最见于处世判事之际。

For expert and execute, and perhaps judge of particulars, one by one; but the general counsels, and the plots and marshalling of affairs, come best form those that are learned. To spend too much time in studies is sloth; to use them too much for ornament, is affectation; to make judgement wholly by their rules, is the humour of a scholar.

练达之士虽能分别处理细事或一一判别枝节,然纵观统筹,全局策划,则舍好学深思者莫属。读书费时过多易惰,文采藻饰太盛则矫,全凭条文断事乃学究故态。

They perfect nature, and are perfected by experience: for natural abilities are like natural plants, that need proyning by study; and studies themselves do give forth directions too much at large, except they be bounded in by experience.

读书补天然之不足,经验又补读书之不足,盖天生才干犹如自然花草,读书然后知如何修剪移接,而书中所示,如不以经验范之,则又大而无当。

Crafty men contemn studies, simple men admire them, and wise men use them; for they teach not their own use; but that is a wisdom without them, and above them, won by observation.

有一技之长者鄙读书,无知者羡读书,唯明智之士用读书,然书并不以用处告人,用书之智不在书中,而在书外,全凭观察得之。

Read not to contradict and confute; nor to believe and take for granted; nor to find talk and discourse; but to weigh and consider.

读书时不可存心诘难作者,不可尽信书上所言,亦不可只为寻章摘句,而应推敲细思。

Some books are to be tasted, others to be swallowed, and some few to be chewed and digested; that is, some books are to be read only in parts; others to be read, but not curiously; and some few to be read wholly, and with diligence and attention.

书有可浅尝者,有可吞食者,少数则须咀嚼消化。换言之,有只需读其部分者,有只需大体涉猎者,少数则须全读,读时须全神贯注,孜孜不倦。

Some books also may be read by deputy, and extracts made of them by others; but that would be only in the less important arguments, and the meaner sort of books; else distilled books are, like common distilled waters, flashy things.

书亦可请人代读,取其所作摘要,但只限题材较次或价值不高者,否则书经提炼犹如水经蒸馏，淡而无味。

Reading maketh a full man; conference a ready man; and writing an exact man. And therefore, if a man write little, he had need have a great memory; if he confer little, he had need have a present wit; and if he read little, he had need have much cunning, to seem to know that he doth not.

读书使人充实，讨论使人机智，笔记使人准确。因此不常做笔记者须记忆力特强，不常讨论者须天生聪颖，不常读书者须欺世有术，始能无知而显有知。

Histories make men wise; poets witty; the mathematics subtile; natural philosophy deep; moral grave; logic and rhetoric able to contend. Abeunt studia in morse.

读史使人明智，读诗使人灵秀，数学使人周密，科学使人深刻，伦理学使人庄重，逻辑修辞之学使人善辩；凡有所学，皆成性格。

Nay there is no stand or impediment in the wit, but may be wrought out by fit studies: like as diseases of the body may have appropriate exercises. Bowling is good for the stone and reins; shooting for the lungs and breast; gentle walking for the stomach; riding for the head; and the like.

人之才智但有滞碍，无不可读适当之书使之顺畅，一如身体百病，皆可借相宜之运动除之。滚球利睾肾，射箭利胸肺，慢步利肠胃，骑术利头脑，诸如此类。

So if a man's wit be wandering, let him study the mathematics; for in demonstrations, if his wit be called away never so little, he must begin again. If his wit be not apt to distinguish or find differences, let him study the schoolmen; for they are cymini sectores. If he be not apt to beat over matters, and to call up one thing to prove and illustrate another, let him study the lawyers' cases. So every defect of the mind may have a special receipt.

如智力不集中，可令读数学，盖演题需全神贯注，稍有分散即须重演；如不能辨异，可令读经院哲学，盖是辈皆吹毛求疵之人；如不善求同，不善以一物阐证另一物，可令读律师之案卷。如此头脑中凡有缺陷，皆有特效可医。

3. Su Shi's *The Midautumn Festival*

水调歌头 Tune: Prelude to Water Melody

明月几时有？
把酒问青天。
How long will the full moon appear?
Wine cup in hand, I ask the sky.

不知天上宫阙，
今夕是何年？
I do not know what time of the year，
It would be tonight in the palace on high.

我欲乘风归去，
又恐琼楼玉宇，
高处不胜寒。
Riding the wind，there I would fly，
Yet I'm afraid the crystalline palace would be
Too high and cold for me.

起舞弄清影，
何似在人间。
I rise and dance，with my shadow I play.
On high as on earth，would it be as gay?

转朱阁，
低绮户，
照无眠。
The moon goes round the mansions red
Through gauze-draped window soft to shed
Her light upon the sleepless bed.

不应有恨，何事长向别时圆？
Why then when people part，is the oft full and bright?

人有悲欢离合，
月有阴晴圆缺，
此事古难全。
Men have sorrow and joy；they part or meet again；
The moon is bright or dim and she may wax or wane.
There has been nothing perfect since the olden days.

但愿人长久，
千里共婵娟。
So let us wish that man

Will live long as he can!
Though miles apart, we'll share the beauty she displays.

3.6 A Glossary of Literature in English and Chinese

版权，著作权 copyright
报告文学 reportage
悲剧 tragedy
表现主义 expressionism
长篇小说 saga (river) novel
场 scene
畅销书 best seller
超现实主义 surrealism
抽象派，抽象主义 abstract art
存在主义 existentialism
错综复杂的剧情 intrigue
达达主义 Dadaism
大众文学 popular literature
短篇小说 short story
古典文学 classical literature
古典主义，古典风格 classicism
故事 story
怪诞小说 mystery story
滑稽剧 farce
话剧 drama
杰作 masterpiece
结局 ending, denouement
精装 deluxe binding
剧本 play
科幻，科学幻想小说 science fiction
浪漫主义 romanticism
历史小说 historical novel
立体派，立体主义 cubism
民间文学 folklore
幕 act
平装 flat stitching
评论 criticism
情节 plot

全集 the complete works (of)
散文 prose
十四行诗 sonnet
史诗 epic poetry
颂歌 ode
通俗文学 light literature
推理小说 whodunit
未来主义 futurism
喜剧 comedy
戏剧 theatre (美 theater)
现代文学 contemporary literature
现实主义 realism
象征主义 symbolism
新古典主义 neoclassicism
新艺术主义 Art Nouveau
叙事诗 epopee
选集 anthology
野兽派 Fauvism
逸事 episode
印象主义 impressionism
幽默小说 humorous story
游记 book of travels
寓言 allegory
韵脚,押韵 rhyme
韵律学,格律学 metrics
侦破小说 detective story
中篇小说 short novel, long short story
自传 biography
自然主义 naturalism

Chapter 4 Contrast of Sino-Western Cultures and Chinese-English Translation Texts in the Field of Classics

4.1 What Is Classics

Classics (also Classical Studies) is the study of the languages, literature, laws, philosophy, history, art, archaeology and other material culture of Ancient Greece and Ancient Rome; especially during Classical Antiquity (600 BC — AD 600). Traditionally, the study of classical literature (Greek and Roman) was the principal study of the humanities.

In this book, classics is analogically broadened to encompass the Chinese classic texts of the pre-Qin era, i. e. the Spring and Autumn Period and the Warring States Period, which is known for the contending scholars, each producing a competing school of theory reminiscent of the Chinese idiom of *letting one hundred flowers to bloom and letting one hundred schools of thoughts to contend*.

Buddhist scriptures, imported and translated at a much later stage (from East Han onward), are conventionally counted as Chinese classics. As a consequence, Confucianism, Buddhism and Taoism have become the three integral parts of Chinese classics.

4.2 Cultural Contrast of Classics of China and the West

4.2.1 Classics of China

Classics of China refers to the Chinese texts which originated before the imperial unification by the Qin dynasty in 221 BC, particularly the "Four Books and Five Classics" of the Neo-Confucian tradition, themselves a customary abridgment of the "Thirteen Classics." All of these pre-Qin texts were written in classical Chinese.

In the Ming and Qing dynasties, the Four Books and Five Classics were the subject of mandatory study by those Confucian scholars who wished to take the imperial exams to become government officials.

The Four Books are:

The Great Learning; *The Doctrine of the Mean*; *The Analects of Confucius*; *The*

Mencius.

The Five Classics are:

The Classic of Poetry; *The Classic of History* or *Book of Documents*; *The I Ching* or *Book of Changes*; *The Classic of Rites*; *The Spring and Autumn Annals*.

The Classics of Taoism:

Tao Te Ching, attributed to Laozi; *Zhuangzi*, attributed to the philosopher of the same name, Zhuangzi; *The Liezi* or *Classic of the Perfect Emptiness*, attributed to Lie Yukou.

The Classic of Mohism:

Mozi, attributed to the philosopher of the same name, Mozi.

The Classics of Legalism:

The Book of Lord Shang, attributed to Shang Yang; *Guanzi*, attributed to Guan Zhong; *Hanfeizi*, attributed to Han Fei.

The Classics of Military Science:

The Art of War, attributed to Sunzi; *The Thirty-Six Stratagems*; *The Three Strategies of Huang Shigong*, attributed to Jiang Ziya.

The first documented translation of Buddhist scriptures from various Indian languages into Chinese occured in the year of 148 with the arrival of the Parthian (帕提亚人) prince-turned-monk An Shigao (安世高). An Xuan (安玄), a Parthian layman who worked alongside An Shigao, also translated an early Mahāyāna Buddhist text(大乘经典).

The celebrated monk in Tang dynasty, Xuanzang (玄奘), is one of the most famous and most prolific translators. He went on foot and endured an incredibly long tour to and back from India and brought back a heavy load of Buddhism scriptures and translated a substantial part throughout the rest of his life.

Names of some widely read Mahāyāna Buddhist scriptures: *Amitabha Sutra*(《阿弥陀经》); *Sukhavati-vyuha*(《无量寿经》); *Amitayur-dhyana-sutra*(《观无量寿经》).

4.2.2 Classics of the West

The classical languages of the Ancient Merranean world influenced every European language, imparting to each a learned vocabulary of international application. Thus, Latin grew from a highly developed cultural product of the Golden and Silver eras of Latin literature to become the international lingua franca in matters diplomatic, scientific, philosophic and religious, until the 17th century.

In turn, the classical languages continued, Latin evolved into the Romance languages and Ancient Greek into Modern Greek and its dialects. In the specialized science and technology vocabularies, the influence of Latin and Greek is notable. Ecclesiastical Latin, the Roman Catholic Church's official tongue, remains a living legacy of the classical world to the contemporary world.

There is a surviving tradition of Latin philology in Western culture connecting the Roman Empire with the Early Modern period. The philology of Greek survived in the Byzantine Empire until the fall of Constantinople, and was re-introduced in Western Europe in the Renaissance.

Classical philology was a major preoccupation of the 19th-century German education system, which became "the paradigm for higher education" throughout Western culture.

One definition of classical philology describes it as "the science which concerns itself with everything that has been transmitted from antiquity in the Greek or Latin language. The object of this science is thus the Graeco-Roman, or Classical, world to the extent that it has left behind monuments in a linguistic form" or alternatively as "the careful study of the literary and philosophical texts of the ancient Greek and Roman worlds."

Classical archaeology is the investigation of the physical remains of the great Merranean civilizations of Ancient Greece and Ancient Rome. Some art historians focus their study of the development of art on the classical world.

4.3 Chinese-English Translation Texts in the Field of Classics

4.3.1 Considering the Content in Translating the Titles of Classics

The British clergyman James Legge (1815—1897) was an outstanding sinologist and professor in Oxford University. He translated the title of 四书 as The Four Books: *Confucian Analects* (《论语》), *The Great Learning* (《大学》), *The Doctrine of the Mean* (《中庸》) and *The Works of Mencius* (《孟子》). In 1885, *The Li Ki* (《礼记》) appeared in the book market in London. The translation of these books has been very popular since their publication.

Around the turn of the 19th century, Professor Gu Hongming (辜鸿铭, 1857—1928) from Peking University tried his hand at the re-translation of the classics. The books were renamed as *The Discourses and Sayings of Confucius* (《论语》), *The Universal Order* (《中庸》). Later,《大学》was termed *The Great Learning*. Gu's translation was successful because the titles became more transparent: readers can see through what the respective classic is about. Later, Xu Yuanchong (许渊冲, 1921—) translated《诗经》as *The Book of Songs* and is widely acclaimed because his switch of focus from *poem* (诗) to *song* (歌) is a daring new try and conforms to the classic's content. Similarly,《中庸》develops ancient

Chinese people's value of staying in the middle or remain mean so it is translated into *The Doctrine of the Mean* or *The Golden Mean*, each well reflecting its content.

4.3.2 Considering Differences in Thinking Modes

The previous section focuses on the content of the classic at stake, a change of perspective to the target language and culture will bring about new criteria for judgment. For example, 人无远虑,必有近忧 is a proverb extracted from *The Discourses and Sayings of Confucius* (《论语》), a literal translation can be like this:

> If a man does not give thought to problems which are still distant, he will have worries close at hand.

Chinese readers will feel it good enough, but a closer look at the logical law in it will reveal that it is problematic: there is no cause-effect connection between the two clauses, that is, a man not giving thought to problems which are still distant will not necessarily bring about worries close at hand. Worries are not something mysterious and will not appear from nowhere just because some magic conditions are present. It cannot be denied that the Chinese people are not interested in clarifying the logical law and are satisfied with a fuzzy thought. Such a thinking mode is not without merit but is truly hazardous in theoretical reasoning: this may partially account for the lagging behind of China's natural sciences in history, especially in the past few centuries. A new translation as follows is more acceptable:

> If a man does not give thought to problems which are still distant, he will be worried by them when they come close at hand.

4.3.3 Proper Use of Footnotes in Translation

Cultural shock is a frightening metaphor: when cultural differences are big enough they will bring about the breakdown of cross-cultural communication as a man falls down without consciousness. Ways to guard against cultural shock are multifold. In translating classics, footnotes can be added to make clear what lies hidden between the lines.

Lau (1979: 85) translated the passage 子见南子 taken from《论语·雍也篇第六》as follows:

> The Master went to see Nan Tzu. Tzu-lu was displeased. The Master swore "If I have done anything improper may Heaven's curse be on me, may Heaven's curse be on me!"

English readers will be ignorant of Nan Tzu and her social status or personalities, so cultural shock looms large. Thanks to Lau's footnote, the crisis dissolved: Nan Tzu is the notorious wife of Duke Ling of Wei.

4.4 Samples

Samples in this section are composed of three origins: Confucianism, Buddhism, and Taoism. These are loosely dubbed three religions which collectively shape the Chinese culture and the personality of the Chinese known to possess a Confucian look, a Buddhist heart and a Taoist way of life.

1. Samples of Confucian Classics: Lines from *The Analects*

子曰:"学而时习之,不亦说乎?有朋自远方来,不亦乐乎?人不知而不愠,不亦君子乎?"

The Master said, "Isn't it a pleasure to learn and constantly practice what is learnt? Isn't it delightful to have friends coming from afar? Isn't he a gentleman who is not annoyed for not being understood?"

子谓韶:"尽美矣,又尽善也;"谓武:"尽美矣,未尽善也。"

The Master evaluated the music Shao, saying, "It is perfectly beautiful, and perfectly good." Then to the music Wu he said, "it is perfectly beautiful, but not perfectly good."

子曰:"不仁者不可以久处约,不可以长处乐。仁者安仁,知者利仁。"

The Master said, "The virtueless cannot live for long either in poverty or in enjoyment. The virtuous devote their minds to benevolent conducts; the wise make the most of their benevolent conducts."

子曰:"贫而无怨难,富而无骄易。"

The Master said, "It's hard to be poor without making complaints. It is easier to be rich without being arrogant."

子曰:"可与言而不与之言,失人;不可与言而与言,失言。知者不失人,亦不失言。"

The Master said, "Failing to talk with a man you ought to talk with might mean losing a friend. Talking with a man you ought not to talk with means saying what you ought not to say. A wise man will neither lose a friend nor utter a wrong word."

子曰:"不在其位,不谋其政。"曾子曰:"君子思不出其位。"

The Master said, "He who does not hold the position shall not involve himself in its affairs." "A superior man does not exceed his authority when he takes an issue into account," added Zengzi.

子曰："孟之反不伐，奔而殿，将入门，策其马，曰：非敢后也，马不进也。"

The Master said, "Meng Zhifan doesn't boast. Once when they lost a battle and retreated, he acted as the rearguard. They were about to enter the city gate when he whipped up his horse to rush ahead, and then said, 'Not that I was brave enough to be the rearguard, but that my horse didn't run fast enough.'"

子曰："后生可畏，焉知来者之不如今也？四十、五十而无闻焉，斯亦不足畏也已。"

The Master said, "Young people are a worthy challenge. Who says that the younger generation will not be as good as the older? But those who still haven't made their mark in their forties or fifties will deserve no reverence."

2. **Buddhist Scripture: *Heart Sutra*** (《心经》)

观自在菩萨，行深般若波罗蜜多，时照见五蕴皆空，度一切苦厄。

Avalokita, the Holy Lord and Bodhisattva, was moving in the deep course of the Wisdom which has gone beyond. He looked down from on high, He beheld but five heaps, and He saw that in their own-being they were empty.

舍利子，色不异空，空不异色，色即是空，空即是色，受想行识，亦复如是。

Here, O Sariputra, form is emptiness and the very emptiness is form; emptiness does not differ from form, form does not differ from emptiness, whatever is emptiness, that is form, the same is true of feelings, perceptions, impulses, and consciousness.

舍利子，是诸法空相，不生不灭，不垢不净，不增不减。

Here, O Sariputra, all dharmas are marked with emptiness; they are not produced or stopped, not defiled or immaculate, not deficient or complete.

是故空中无色，无受想行识，无眼耳鼻舌身意，无色声香味触法。无眼界，乃至无意识界。无无明，亦无无明尽，乃至无老死，亦无老死尽。

Therefore, O Sariputra, in emptiness there is no form nor feeling, nor perception, nor impulse, nor consciousness; No eye, ear, nose, tongue, body, mind; No forms, sounds, smells, tastes, touchables or objects of mind; No sight-organ element, and so forth, until we come to: No mind-consciousness element; There is no ignorance, no extinction of ignorance, and so forth, until we come to: There is no decay and death, no extinction of decay and death.

无苦集灭道，无智亦无得。

There is no suffering, no origination, no stopping, no path. There is no cognition, no attainment and no non-attainment.

以无所得故，菩提萨埵。依般若波罗蜜多故，心无罣(guà)碍。

Therefore, O Sariputra, it is because of his non-attainmentness that a Bodhisattva, through having relied on the Perfection of Wisdom, dwells without thought-coverings.

无罣碍故，无有恐怖。远离颠倒梦想，究竟涅磐。

In the absence of thought-coverings he has not been made to tremble, he has overcome what can upset, and in the end he attains to Nirvana.

三世诸佛，依般若波罗蜜多故，得阿耨(nòu)多罗三藐三菩提。

All those who appear as Buddhas in the three periods of time fully awake to the utmost, right and perfect Enlightenment because they have relied on the Perfection of Wisdom.

故知般若波罗蜜多，是大神咒，是大明咒，是无上咒，是无等等咒，能除一切苦，真实不虚。

Therefore one should know the prajnaparamita as the great spell, the spell of great knowledge, the utmost spell, the unequalled spell, allayer of all suffering, in truth — for what could go wrong?

故说般若(bō rě)波罗蜜多咒，即说咒曰：揭谛！揭谛！波罗揭谛！波罗僧揭谛！菩提萨婆诃！

By the prajnaparamita has this spell been delivered. It runs like this: gate gate paragate parasamgate bodhi svaha.

3. *Tao Te Ching* (excerpt)

道可道，非常道；名可名，非常名。无名，天地之始；有名，万物之母。故常无欲，以观其妙；常有欲，以观其徼。此两者，同出而异名，同谓之玄。玄之又玄，众妙之门。

The Way that can be told of is not an Unvarying Way; The names that can be named are not unvarying names. It was from the Nameless that Heaven and Earth sprang; The named is but the mother that rears the ten thousand creatures, each after its kind. Truly, "Only he that rids himself forever of desire can see the Secret Essences"; He that has never rid himself of desire can see only the Outcomes. These two things issued from the same mould, but nevertheless are different in name. This "same mould" we can but call the Mystery, or rather the "Darker than any Mystery", the Doorway whence issued all Secret Essences.

天下皆知美之为美，斯恶已；皆知善之为善，斯不善已。故有无相生，难易相成，长短相形，高下相倾，音声相和，前后相随。是以圣人处无为之事，行不言之教，万物作焉而不辞，生而不有，为而不恃，功成而弗居。夫唯弗居，是以不去。

It is because every one under Heaven recognizes beauty as beauty, that the idea of ugliness exists. And equally if every one recognized virtue as virtue, this would merely create fresh conceptions of wickedness. For truly being and not-being grow out of one another; difficult and easy complete one another. Long and short test one another; high and low determine one another. Pitch and mode give harmony to one another; front and back give sequence to one another. Therefore the Sage relies on actionless activity, carries on wordless teaching, but the myriad creatures are worked upon by him, and he does not disown them. He rears them, but does not lay claim to them; controls them, but does not lean upon them; achieves his aim, but does not call attention to what he does. And for the very reason that he does not call attention to what he does, he is not ejected from the fruition of what he has done.

不尚贤，使民不争；不贵难得之货，使民不为盗；不见可欲，使民心不乱。是以圣人之治，虚其心，实其腹；弱其志，强其骨。常使民无知无欲，使夫智者不敢为也。为无为，则无不治。

If we stop looking for "persons of superior morality" to put in power, there will be no more jealousies among the people. If we cease to set store by products that are hard to get, there will be no more thieves. If the people never see such things as excite desire, their hearts will remain placid and undisturbed. Therefore the Sage rules by emptying their hearts and filling their bellies, weakening their intelligence and toughening their sinews, striving to make the people knowledgeless and desireless. Indeed he sees to it that if there be any who have knowledge, they dare not interfere. Yet through his actionless activity all things are duly regulated.

道冲而用之，或不盈。渊兮，似万物之宗。挫其锐，解其纷，和其光，同其尘。湛兮，似或存。吾不知谁之子，象帝之先。

The Way is like an empty vessel that yet may be drawn from without ever needing to be filled. It is bottomless; the very progenitor（祖先）of all things in the world. In it all sharpness is blunted, all tangles untied, all glare tempered, all dust smoothed. It is like a deep pool that never dries. Was it too the child of something else? We cannot tell. But as a substanceless image it existed before the Ancestor.

天地不仁，以万物为刍狗；圣人不仁，以百姓为刍狗。天地之间，其犹橐籥乎！虚而不屈，动而愈出。多言数穷，不如守中。

Heaven and Earth are feelingless; to them all things are but as straw dogs. The Sage too is feelingless; to him the people are but as straw dogs. Nature lies between Heaven and Earth like a bellows that is empty, but it gives a supply that never fails. Work it, and more comes out. Whereas the force of words is soon spent, far better is it to keep what is in the heart.

谷神不死,是谓玄牝。玄牝之门,是谓天地根。绵绵若存,用之不勤。

The Void Spirit never dies. It is named the Mysterious Female. And the Doorway of the Mysterious Female is the base from which Heaven and Earth sprang. It is there within us all the while;Draw upon it as you will,it never runs dry.

天长地久,天地所以能长且久者,以其不自生,故能长生。是以圣人后其身而身先,外其身而身存。非以其无私邪? 故能成其私。

Heaven is eternal,the Earth everlasting. How come they to be so? Is it because they do not foster their own lives? That is why they live so long. Therefore the Sage puts himself in the background, but is always to the fore; remains outside, but is always there. Is it not just because he does not strive for any personal end that all his personal ends are fulfilled?

上善若水,水善利万物而不争。处众人之所恶,故几于道。居善地,心善渊,与善仁,言善信,正善治,事善能,动善时。夫唯不争,故无尤。

The highest good is like that of water. The goodness of water is that it benefits ten thousand creatures; yet it does not scramble for itself, but is content with the places that all men disdain. It is this that makes water so near to the Way. And if men think the ground the best place for building a house upon; if among thoughts they value those that are profound; if in friendship they value gentleness; in words, truth; in government, good order; in deeds, effectiveness; in actions, timelines—in each case it is because they prefer what does not lead to strife, and therefore do not go amiss.

4.5 A Glossary of Chinese Classics in English and Chinese

《春秋》*The Spring and Autumn Annals*

《大学》*The Great Learning*

《道德经》*Tao Te Ching/Classic of the Way of Virtue*

《国策》*Discourses of the States*

《离骚》*Sorrow after Departure*

《礼记》*The Book of Rites*

《论语》*The Analects of Confucius*

《孟子》*The Words of Mencius*

《山海经》*Mountain and Sea Classics*

《诗经》*The Book of Songs*

《史记》*Records of the Historian*
《书经》*The Book of History*
《易经》*The Book of Changes*
《战国策》*Strategies of the Warring States*
《中庸》*The Doctrine of the Mean*
《左传》*The Spring and Autumn Annals*
《阿弥陀经》*Amitabha Sutra*
《长阿含经》*Dirhagama*
《地藏经》*Sutra of Past Vows of Earth Store (Di Zang) Budhisattva*
《观无量寿经》*Amitayur-dhyana Sutra*
《金刚经》*Vajracchedikā-prajñāpāramitā Sūtra*
《楞严经》*Śūraṃgama-sutra*
《妙法莲华经》 *Lotus Sutra*
《无量寿经》*Sukhavati-vyuha*
《心经》*Heart Sutra*
《杂阿含经》*Samyuktagama*
《中阿含经》*Madhyamagama*

Chapter 5 Contrast of Sino-Western Cultures and Chinese-English Translation Texts in the Field of Film

5.1 What Is Film

A film is a series of still images which, when shown on a screen, creates the illusion of moving images. This optical illusion causes the audience to perceive continuous motion between separate objects viewed rapidly in succession.

The word *cinema*, short for cinematography, is often used to refer to the industry of film, film-making or the art of filmmaking itself.

The contemporary definition of cinema is the art of simulating experiences to communicate ideas, stories, perceptions, feelings, beauty or atmosphere by means of recorded or programmed moving images along with other sensory stimulations.

5.2 Cultural Contrast of Film in China and the West

5.2.1 Film in China

Motion pictures were introduced to China in 1896. The first recorded screening of motion picture in China occurred in Shanghai in 1896. The first Chinese film, a recording of the Beijing Opera, *The Battle of Dingjunshan*, was made in 1905. During the 1920s film technicians from the United States trained Chinese technicians in Shanghai, and American influence continued to be felt there for the next two decades.

Since the founding of the PRC in 1949, the number of movie-viewers increased sharply. Beginning in the mid-late 1980s, the rise of the so-called Fifth Generation of Chinese filmmakers brought increased popularity of Chinese cinema abroad.

The recent era has seen the "return of the amateur filmmaker" loosely referred to as the Sixth Generation. These films are shot quickly and cheaply, which produce a documentary feel: long takes, hand-held cameras, ambient sound. Many films are joint ventures and projects with international investment. Unlike the Fifth Generation, the Sixth Generation brings a more individualistic, anti-romantic life-view and pays more attention to contemporary urban life, especially affected by disorientation.

5.2.2 Film in the West

The United Kingdom has had a significant film industry for over a century. While film production reached an all-time high in 1936, the "golden age" of British cinema is usually thought to have occurred in the 1940s. Many British actors have achieved international fame and critical success, including Maggie Smith, Michael Caine, Sean Connery and Kate Winslet. Some of the films with the largest ever box office returns have been made in the United Kingdom, including the second and third highest-grossing film series (*Harry Potter* and *James Bond*).

In the United States, Hollywood has had a profound effect on cinema across the world since the early 20th century. The dominant style of American cinema is Classical Hollywood Cinema, which developed from 1917 to 1960 and characterizes most films to this day. The major film studios of Hollywood are the primary source of the most commercially successful movies in the world, such as *Gone with the Wind* (1939), *Star Wars* (1977), *Titanic* (1997), *Avatar* (2009), *The Avengers* (2012), *Furious 7* (2015), *Jurassic World* (2015) and *Star Wars: The Force Awakens* (2015). Today, American film studios collectively generate several hundred movies every year, making the United States one of the most prolific producers of films in the world.

5.3 Chinese-English Translation Texts in the Field of Film

5.3.1 Techniques in the Translation of Film Titles

A good film should successfully attract the viewer's attention to make money or publicize something. Before actually watching a film, the potential viewers make their decisions on the basis of the title of the film. So film directors will spare no effort to modify the title of their films. However, a good title in one language may not turn out to be alluring to potential viewers in another language; this puts a high demand on the part of the translator. For example, shoot-outs films (警匪片) beat their peers by suspenses and fierce fightings, which are often reflected in their titles or the translated titles.

Good examples of translation are fiscally successful ones, but they are never word-for-word translations. Please note the following examples, which are transaltions from English into Chinese. The target language is more fantastic than the source:

《生死时速》: Speed

《石破天惊》: The Rock

《魂断蓝桥》: Waterloo Bridge

《廊桥遗梦》: The Bridges of Madison County

《钢琴别恋》: The Piano

《人鬼情未了》: Ghost

《克雷默夫妇》: Kramer vs Kramer

《蝙蝠侠》: Batman

《侏罗纪公园》: Jurassic Park

《星球大战》: Star Wars

《阿甘正传》: Forrest Gump

《未来战士》: Terminator

《罗马假日》: Roman Holiday

《窈窕淑女》: My Fair Lady

《金色池塘》: On the Golden Pond

《出水芙蓉》: Bathing Beauty

It is obvious that the examples above are very brief, and most of them coincide with an idiom. Brevity is the soul of wit. It is not a hard thing to translate a short title into a concise counterpart; it is real smart to translate a lengthy title into a phonologically and lexically concentrated one. The following are examples:

《性爱宝典》: Everything You Always Wanted to Know About Sex But Afraid to Ask

《双姝奇恋》: The Incredibly True Adventures of Two Girls in Love

The film *The Englishman Who Went Up a Hill But Came Down a Mountain* was first translated into《上山又下山的英国人》. The Chinese title is much shorter than its counterpart, but it is still defective in that the English title stresses the contrast of *hill* and *mountain*, but their differences are neglected when they appear respectively in 上山 and 下山. Later《神圣的大山》replaced《上山又下山的英国人》, achieving the utmost in brevity and semantic robustness.

The film *North by Northwest* can be readily translated into《北西北》or《西北偏北》as their dictionary meanings suggest, but the translations are hardly intelligible to Chinese reader. A conscientious consideration of its theme brings forth the best name《谍海疑云》. Similar examples can be found in the translations from *Hamlet* into《王子复仇记》, *Oliver Twist* into《雾都孤儿》and *Gone with the Wind* into《乱世佳人》.

5.3.2 Integrating the Actor's Lines with the Hero's State of Mind

In translating the actor's or actress's lines, literal translation often fails. The hero's state of mind must be intergrated with the lines, so adjustments must be made to meet the situation in the film. Let's cite some examples from the film *Caroline* (《鬼妈妈》):

(1) C: I don't like being stalked, not by psycho nerds or their cats!

我可不喜欢被跟踪,不喜欢被个神经病还有他的猫跟踪。

W: He's not really my cat, he's kind of feral. You know, wild.

它又不是我的猫,还有点凶凶的,野猫嘛。

In (1), Caroline's line *psycho nerds or their cats* uses plural form, which refer to people or stuff of some particular kind, just like *horses are useful animals* meaning that the species of horse is a useful animal. The Chinese translation renders the plural form into singular, 个神经病还有他的猫. Singular form in Chinese can better reveal Caroline's psychology of focused disgust pointing to particular referent.

The next line *not really my cat, kind of feral. You know, wild* is translated into 又不是我的猫，还有点凶凶的，野猫嘛. Chinese readers can feel the tenderness in her voice. Tenderness comes from her desire for reconciliation and freedom from misunderstanding.

(2) C: I would've died.
我差点就没命了。
RM: That's nice.
太好了。
C: Hmm. So can I go out? I think it's perfect weather for gardening.
嗯。我能出去吗？天气这么好，真适合种花。
RM: No, Caroline. Rain makes mud. Mud makes a mess.
不行，卡萝兰。下雨就有泥巴，泥巴会弄得你全身脏兮兮。
C: But, Mom, I want stuff growing when my friends come to visit.
妈咪，我想要等到朋友们来的时候，我花园里的花都盛开起来。
C: I can't believe it. You and dad get paid to write about plants, and you hate dirt.
我真不敢相信。你和爸爸靠写植物特性来赚钱，而你却讨厌泥巴。
RM: Caroline, I don't have time for you right now.
卡萝兰，我现在没时间陪你闹。

In (2), Caroline was anxious for love and care from her parents who were very busy and could hardly afford the time. When it rained, Caroline wanted to go out to do the gardening, but was refused by her mother. Disappointment and frustration occupied Caroline at that moment. This was fully considered in the translator's conversion of the words between English and Chinese:

1. The abstract concepts of *gardening* and *stuff* are converted into concrete concepts 种花 and 花;
2. The concrete *plants* becomes abstract 植物特性;
3. The noun *rain* in *Rain makes mud* becomes a verb 下雨;
4. The fuzzy word *mess* changes into the clarified phrase 你全身;
5. The phrase *don't have time for* is augmented into 没时间陪……闹.

(3) C: A little me? That's weird.
是我的迷你版？真是太诡异了。

RM：What's his name，anyway?
他叫什么？
C：Wybie. And I'm way too old for dolls.
韦伯。我再玩洋娃娃就太装嫩了。

When Caroline was given the dolls，she responded *I'm way too old for dolls*. If literally put，我已经过了玩洋娃娃的年纪了 is a plain remark and cannot show her good humor，while 我再玩洋娃娃就太装嫩了 is an intelligent response and reveals her state of mind：she was not yet an adult but too old for doll. 玩洋娃娃就太装嫩 is a mimic of the tone of someone who is much older than her and therefore carries some humorous flavor.

5.4 Samples

Lines quoted from Antoine de Saint-Exupéry's *The Little Prince*：

If someone loves a flower，of which just one single blossom grows in all the millions and millions of stars，it is enough to make him happy just to look at the stars. He can say to himself，"Somewhere，my flower is there..." But if the sheep eats the flower，in one moment all his stars will be darkened... And you think that is not important!

倘若一个人对一朵花情有独钟，而那花在浩瀚的星河中，是独一无二的，那么，他只要仰望繁星点点，就心满意足了。他会喃喃自语："我的花就在星河的某个角落……"可是，这花一旦被羊吃掉了，一瞬间，所有星星都将随之黯淡无光…… 那你也认为这不重要吗？

My flower is ephemeral，and she has only four thorns to defend herself against the world. And I have left her on my planet，all alone!

我的花生命是短暂的，她只有四根刺可以保护自己，抵御世界，我却将她独自留在我的星球上了！

His flower had told him that she was only one of her kind in all universe. And here were five thousand of them，all alike，in one single garden!

他的花朵曾经告诉他，自己是宇宙间仅有的一种花；可是仅仅在这座花园里，就有五千朵和她一模一样的花！

I thought that I was rich，with a flower that was unique in all the world；and all I had was a common rose. A common rose...

我总以为自己很富有，拥有一朵世上独一无二的花；实际上，我所拥有的不过是一朵普通的玫瑰而已。一朵普通的玫瑰花……

To me，you are still nothing more than a little boy who is just like a hundred thousand other little boys. And I have no need of you. And you, on your part, have no need of me. To you, I am nothing more than a fox like a hundred thousand other foxes. But if you tame me, then we shall need each other. To me, you will be unique in all the world. To you, I shall be unique in all the world.

对我而言,你只是一个小男孩,和其他成千上万的小男孩没有什么不同。我不需要你。你也不需要我。对你而言,我也和其它成千上万的狐狸并没有差别。但是,假如你驯服了我,我们就彼此需要了。对我而言,你就是举世无双的;对你而言,我也是独一无二的。

The wheat fields have nothing to say to me. And that is sad. But you have hair that is the color of gold. Think how wonderful that will be when you have tamed me! The grain, which is also golden, will bring me back the thought of you. And I shall love to listen to the wind in the wheat.

麦田和我毫不相干,真令人沮丧。不过,你有金黄色的头发。想想看,如果你驯服了我,那该有多好啊!小麦也是金黄色的,那会使我想起你。我会喜欢听麦田里的风声。

It is your own fault, I never wished you any sort of harm; but you wanted me to tame you... but now you are going to cry! Then it has done you no good at all!

这是你的错,我根本无意伤害你,可是你却愿意让我驯服你…… 可是你现在却想哭!那驯服根本对你毫无好处!

It has done me good, because of the color of the wheat fields. Go and look again at the roses. You will understand now that yours is unique in all the world.

驯服对我是有好处的——因为麦田的颜色。再回头看那些玫瑰花吧!到时你就明白你的玫瑰花仍是举世无双的一朵花。

And now here is my secret, a very simple secret. It is only with the heart that one can see rightly; what is essential is invisible to the eyes.

这是我的一个秘密,再简单不过的秘密:一个人只有用心去看,才能看到真实。事情的真相只用眼睛是看不见的。

Men have forgotten this truth. But you must not forget it. You become responsible, forever, for what you have tamed. You are responsible for your rose...

人们早已忘记了这个道理。可是你不应将它遗忘。你必须永远对自己所驯服的东西负责。你要对你的玫瑰花负责。

Only the children know what they are looking for. They waste their time over a rag doll and it becomes very important to them; and if anybody takes it away from them, they cry...

只有小孩子知道自己在找什么。他们把时间花费在布娃娃身上。因此对他们而言，洋娃娃就变得很重要。一旦有人将娃娃拿走，他们就会号啕大哭……

What moves me so deeply, about this little prince who is sleeping here, is his loyalty to a flower — the image of a rose that shine through his whole being like the flame of a lamp, even when he is asleep...

这个熟睡的小王子最叫我感动的地方是，他对一朵玫瑰的感情——甚至他睡着了，那朵玫瑰花的影子，仍像灯光一样照亮他的生命……

The men where you live, raise five thousand roses in the same garden — and they do not find in it what they are looking for. And yet what they are looking for could be found in one single rose, or in a little water. But eyes are blind. One must look with the heart...

你所居住的星球上的人们，在同一座花园培育了五千朵玫瑰——却无法从中找到他们所要寻找的东西。但是，他们所寻找的，其实是可以从一朵玫瑰花或一滴水中找到的。然而眼睛往往是盲从的。人还是必须用心去看……

All men have the stars, but they are not the same things for different people. For some, who are travelers, the stars are guides. For others they are no more than little lights in the sky. For others, who are scholars, they are problems. For my businessman they were wealth. But all these stars are silent. You — you alone — will have the stars as no one else has them...

每一个人都有自己的星星，但其中的含义却因人而异。对旅人而言，星星是向导；对其他人而言，它们只不过是天际中闪闪发光的小东西而已；对学者而言，星星则是待解的难题；对我那位商人来说，它们就是财富。不过，星星本身是沉默的。你——只有你——了解这些星星与众不同的含义……

And when your sorrow is comforted (time soothes all sorrows) you will be content that you have known me. You will always be my friend. You will want to laugh with me. And you will sometimes open your window, so, for that pleasure... And your friends will be properly astonished to see you laughing as you look up at the sky! Then you will say to them, "Yes, the stars always make me laugh!"

当你不再感到伤心的时候(时间会冲淡一切伤痛)，你就会因认识我而感到心满意足。你是我永远的朋友。将会和我一起欢笑。为了欢乐，你会经常打开窗子…… 当你的朋友看到你因仰望天空而大笑时，一定会感到莫名其妙！到时候，你可以对他们说："是的，星星总让我开心而笑！"

5.5 A Glossary of Film in English and Chinese

暴力派动画 animation school of violence

背景音乐 background music
表演场次 action cutting
表演区 action field
玻璃接景法 glass shot
插曲 interlude
冲击蒙太奇 montage of collision
导片 leader
导演 director
倒叙 flash-back
盗匪片 gangster film
登山片 mountain film
殿堂导演 pantheon director
动画设计 animator
动画摄影机 animation camera
动画摄影台 animation stand
动作连戏 match on action
动作片 action film
独立制片 independent filmmaking
对白配音 dubbing
对嘴 lip sync
非剧情片 nonfiction film
非摄影电影 non-camera film
非戏院电影 nontheatrical film
好莱坞 Hollywood
黑色电影 film noir
横摇镜头 pan
幻想片 fantasy film
即兴台词 ad lib
纪录剧情片 docudrama
纪实片 actualite
剪接 editing,cutting
剪接师 editor
经纪人 agent
镜头内剪接 in-camera editing
剧情片 feature film
卡通片 cartoon
开拍 action
恐怖片 horror film

立体电影 anaglyph
联合制片人 associate producer
露天汽车电影院 drive-in theater
卖座率 audience rating
美国式蒙太奇 American montage
美术设计 art direction
美术指导 art director
蒙太奇 montage
前卫电影 avant-garde
情调音乐 mood music
全息摄影 holography
热接片法 hot splice
摄影师 camera operator
摄影师 cameraman
摄影指导 director of photography
生活化影片 flow-of-film
实景拍摄 location shooting
史诗纪录片 epic documentary
收视率 audience share
提示字幕 capion
替身 double
跳切 jump cut
通俗剧 melodrama
偷拍 candid camera
透光广告牌 marquee
外景拍摄 location shooting
无痕迹剪接 invisible cutting
吸引力蒙太奇 montage of attraction
香味电影 aromarama
新闻片 newsreel
新写实主义 neorealism
叙事蒙太奇 narrative montage
选角指导 casting director
演员工作室 actor studio
异步声 asynchronous sound
意象派电影 imagist film
音画分立 asynchronism
音乐声带 music track

游说式纪录片 persuasive documentary
预叙 flash-forward
运动摄影 fluid camera
灾难片 disaster film
知性蒙太奇 intellectual montage
主镜头 master shot, master scene
资讯影片 information film

Chapter 6 Contrast of Sino-Western Cultures and Chinese-English Translation Texts in the Field of Journalism

6.1 What Is Journalism

Journalism is the collecting, processing, and dissemination of news, and information related to news, to an audience. The word applies to the method of inquiring for news, the literary style which is used to disseminate it, and the activity of journalism.

In modern society, the news media is the chief purveyor of information and opinion about public affairs. Journalism, however, is not always confined to the news media or to news itself, as journalistic communication may find its way into broader forms of expression, including literature and cinema.

News style (also journalistic style or news writing style) is the prose style used for news reporting in media such as newspapers, radio and television. News style encompasses not only vocabulary and sentence structure, but also the way in which stories present the information in terms of relative importance, tone, and intended audience.

News writing attempts to answer all the basic questions about any particular event — who, what, when, where and why (the Five Ws) and also often how — at the opening of the article. This form of structure is sometimes called the *inverted pyramid*, to refer to the decreasing importance of information in subsequent paragraphs.

Journalistic prose is explicit and precise, and tries not to rely on jargon. As a rule, journalists will not use a long word when a short one will do. They use subject-verb-object construction and vivid, active prose. They offer anecdotes, examples and metaphors, and they rarely depend on colorless generalizations or abstract ideas. News writers try to avoid using the same word more than once in a paragraph.

6.2 Cultural Contrast of Journalism in China and the West

6.2.1 Journalism in China

The first privately published news sheet appeared in 1582 in Beijing, during the late Ming dynasty. *China Monthly Magazine*, which published from 1815 to 1821, marked the beginning of Chinese journalism. China's first newspaper, the *English-language Canton Register*, was established in 1827.

Chinese-language missionary journalism restarted with *China Serial*, published in Hong Kong from 1853 to 1856. *Wanguo Gongbao* (*A Review of the Times*), the most influential Chinese publication of the 19th century, was published from 1868 to 1907.

Ever since 1949, China has two news agencies, the Xinhua News Agency and the China News Service. Xinhua News Agency is the major source of news and photographs for central and local newspapers.

In 1981 the English language *China Daily* began its publication. This newspaper, which is provided for foreigners living or traveling in China but which also is read by a large number of Chinese literate in English, offers international news and sports from the major foreign wire services as well as interesting domestic news and feature articles.

6.2.2 Journalism in the West

The history of American journalism began in 1690, when Benjamin Harris published *Publick Occurrences, Both Foreign and Domestick* in Boston. Harris intended to publish a regular weekly newspaper along the lines of those that existed in London. The first successful newspaper, *The Boston News-Letter*, was launched in 1704.

As the colonies grew rapidly in the 18th century, new papers appeared in port cities along the East Coast, usually started by master printers seeking a sideline. Among them was James Franklin, founder of *The New England Courant*(《新英格兰报》,1721—1727), where he employed his younger brother, Benjamin Franklin, as a printer's apprentice. Newspapers flourished after the founding of the United States. There were about 234 being published during the early years of its independence.

As American cities like New York, Philadelphia, Boston and Washington grew, so did newspapers. Larger printing presses, the telegraph, and other technological innovations allowed newspapers to print thousands of copies, boost circulation, and increase revenue. In the largest cities some papers were politically independent. But most of them, especially in smaller cities, were closely tied to the political parties, which used them for communication and campaigning.

The first newspaper to fit the 20th century style of a newspaper was *The New York Herald*, founded in 1835 and published by James Gordon Bennett, Sr. It was politically independent, and became the first newspaper to have city staff covering regular beats and spot news, along with regular business and Wall Street coverage. *The New York Times*, now one of the best-known newspapers in the world, was founded in 1851 by George Jones and Henry Raymond. It established the principle of balanced reporting in high-quality writing.

Starting in the 1960s, investigative journalism came back into fashion, as typified by

Bob Woodward and *The Washington Post* exposés of the Watergate scandal. At the local level, the alternative press movement emerged, typified by alternative weekly newspapers like *The Village Voice* in New York City and *The Phoenix* in Boston, as well as political magazines like *Mother Jones* and *The Nation*.

6.3 Chinese-English Translation Texts in the Field of Journalism

Our analysis is based on the following news report published in the bilingual magazine of *China Today* in December 2005:

Title:

少年上人号怀素

The report:

1舞台铺着从中国运来的宣纸，每张长约 6 米，产于安徽，是 20 世纪 70 年代手工制作的产品。2英国大提琴家罗德萨拉(Rohan De Saram)偏坐一隅，身着白衫，双眼微闭，神情笃定，巴赫深沉的大提琴独奏组曲在他的弓下缓缓响起。

3中国书法家曾来德身着唐装，通体缟素，磨墨抚笔，瞑目凝神，在音乐中缓缓进入书写状态。稍顷，落笔纸上，写下中国唐代(618—907)诗人李白所作诗歌《草歌行书》的第一句："少年上人号怀素"。

The title and the report proper are translated as follows:

A Young Monk Named Huaisu

2British cellist Rohan De Saram sits on one side of the stage, his eyes half closed, as he begins to play Bach's Cello Suites. 3Chinese calligrapher Zeng Laide begins grinding his ink stick. He momentarily closes his eyes to focus his concentration, and begins brushing Chinese characters onto 1a 6-meter-long sheet of Xuan paper made in China's Anhui Province in the 1970s. The seven Chinese characters he has written read: "Shaonian shangren hao Huaisu". A young Buddhist monk named Huaisu—the first line of Li Bai's poem *In Praise of Cursive Calligraphy*.

6.3.1 Neglecting the Connotative Meaning of the Source Language

The bilingual news report cited above is well done because it artistically translated some words with a connotation specific to the source language, for example, 上人 is a Buddhist honorary title used to address honorable and generally elderly monks or nuns both in the Tibetan area and Han area. It is translated into *young monk* with much of its appraisal sense filtered away.

It has been part of the Chinese culture to adjust the denotative and connotative meanings of a word out of good manners or pure flattery, for example, in Buddhism, a young monks is generally not lablled 上人 or 师父上人, but 法师 or 和尚 in particular contexts. For a young monk to be addressed 上人 is really something extraordinary.

What is more, 上人 has no equivalent word in the Christian world so it is not easy to be understood by English readers. Neglecting the word 上人 and resorting plainly to the words *young monk* is the best choice.

6.3.2 Readjusting the Word Order of the Source Text

The Chinese mode of thinking is known to be circular or spiral. When the Chinese people speak or write they will not go directly to the theme but try to describe something less relevant to the topic. This is intolerable to English native speakers. In our example cited above, the Chinese version, though it is listed in contrast with the English version, is literally deviating from each other in information (please note the contrast as indicated by the lower case numbers).

The Chinese version begins with a detailed description of the platform, size of the paper, its production location and time. Only when all such trivial information are produced, does the writer bring forth the music player Rohan De Saram whose playing is mingled with the hero's performance of writing.

As a contrast, the English version, though in the same page of the magazine, broadly reshuffles the lines and brings forth the British cellist Rohan De Saram in whose music the Chinese calligrapher demonstrated his good performance of handwriting. It is only behind the main part of the news report does the situation of the platform present itself as a supplement for the background information which is not imperative but may contribute to bringing vividness to the report.

A news report is known to be in the shape of an upside-down pyramid. What appears in the topmost position is the most important part of the story, as it moves down supplementing information of descending importance will take turns to appear so long as space permits. The news report above is a piece of soft news which differs from hard news in that, while the latter is a report of actual relevance to the reader's life such as a war that is going on, or a traffic accident that has just happened somewhere or the worsening price hike, soft news aims to provide some extra knowledge or entertainment for the readers. It is possibly due to its nature of being soft news that the Chinese version differs in the arrangement of news segments.

6.3.3 Addition or Deletion

The Chinese version of the news report, like many other styles of writing, has used many four-character idioms, such as 偏坐一隅，身着白衫，双眼微闭，神情笃定，身着唐装，通体缟素，磨墨抚笔，瞑目凝神，落笔纸上. These idioms read rhythmically and add to the aesthetic effect, but the English version has deleted some of them and simplified some others. New wording patterns are used: *sits on one side of the stage*, *eyes half closed*, *grinding his ink stick*, *momentarily closes his eyes to focus his concentration*, *brushing*, etc.

In the English version, Xuan paper is especially introduced, informing its readers of Xuan paper being made in China's Anhui Province in the 1970s. But the modifier 从中国运来的 is ignored because it is trivial knowledge that, since it belongs to China alone, it is surely made in China.

In the Chinese version, 少年上人号怀素 can be counted and the number is obvious, but when literally spelled in Latin letters, the translator has been so considerate to add *seven Chinese characters* to help English readers to get a clear picture of it.

6.4 Samples

News titles (or Headlines):

Four Saved from Death's Jaws — by a Pod of Dolphins
海豚及时相救,四人死里逃生
Illness prevented him from going there
他因病未能去那里
Women with a university education are choosing to have children later in life, a British research reveals
英国一调查表明,上过大学的女性通常选择晚育
The death toll in flood-ravaged southern Thailand has risen to 439
泰国南方水灾中的死亡人数已经上升到 439 人

Paragraphs cited from some pieces of news:

Emergency talks were held yesterday between the Government and aviation industry representatives to solve an insurance crisis that threatens to ground airlines from tomorrow.

政府和航空界代表昨天举行了紧急会谈,试图解决因保险问题而引发的危机。这场危机会威胁到从明天起起飞的航班。

MANILA (Agencies via Xinhua)—At least 49 people were feared killed and more than 100,000 fled their homes as Typhoon Skip pummeled the Philippines, triggering landslides and floods, officials said yesterday.

新华社马尼拉综合讯——据昨天官方信息,代号为史基普的台风袭击了菲律宾,引发洪水和滑坡,至少造成 49 人死亡,10 万多人流离失所。

Hijackers rammed two jetliners into each of New York's World Trade Center towers yesterday, toppling both in a hellish storm of ash, glass, smoke and leaping victims, while a third jetliner crashed into the Pentagon in Virginia.

几名劫机分子昨日劫持两架喷气式飞机撞向纽约世贸中心,致使南北双塔轰然倒塌,顿时尘土飞扬,玻璃飞溅,浓烟滚滚,人们四处逃生。这一切构成了一幅地狱般的场景。与此同时,第三架飞机又撞击了位于弗吉尼亚州的美国国防部五角大楼。

The Central committee is of the opinion that these reforms should be carried out step by step according to the inherent connections between the various links of the national economy as well as degree of ripening of the subjective and objective conditions and in the right order of importance, urgency and feasibility, and that they should basically be accomplished in about five years.

中央认为,这些改革应根据国民经济各个环节的内在联系和主客观条件的成熟程度,分别轻重缓急和难易,有先有后,逐步进行,争取五年左右的时间基本实现。

6.5 A Glossary of Journalism in English and Chinese

报社 newspaper office
报摊 news stand, kiosk
采访,采写 cover
采访记者 reporter
采写任务 assignment
初任记者 cub reporter
大新闻 flash-news
低俗新闻 yellow sheet
读者来信专栏 correspondence column
发行 distribution
发行人 publisher
分类广告 calssified ad
封面女郎 cover girl
更正(启事) correction
公告 public notice
广告 advertisement
国际新闻协会 International Press Association
号外 extra
坏事传千里 Bad news travels quickly.
记者采访地区 newsbeat
记者席 press box
记者招待会 news conference, press conference

剪辑(图片) crop
禁止刊行 press ban
连载故事,连载小说 continued story
趣闻轶事 anecdote
社长 proprieter
随军记者 war correspondent, campaign badge
桃色新闻,绯闻 affair
特派员 special correspondent
特约编辑 contributing editor
通讯员 correspondent
投稿人 contributor
图片版新闻 tabloid
文艺评论 literary criticism
消息出处,消息来源 attributionn
小道消息 back alley news
新闻背景 backgrounding
新闻编辑部 copydesk
新闻管制 news blackout
新闻记者 newsman, newspaperman, journalist
新闻来源 news source
新闻小说 serial story
新闻战 newspaper campaign
宣传攻势 crusade
隐性采访,秘密采访 covert coverage
预发消息,预写消息 advance
运动栏 the sportspage
周日特刊 Sunday features
驻外记者,常驻外埠记者 correspondent
专栏,栏目 column
专栏记者 columnist
专栏作家 columnist
自由撰稿人 freelance writer
总编辑 bureau chief, copy chief

Chapter 7 Contrast of Sino-Western Cultures and Chinese-English Translation Texts in the Field of Folk Culture

7.1 What Is Folk Culture

Folk culture refers to the unifying expressive components of everyday life as enacted by localized, tradition-bound groups. Earlier conceptualizations of folk culture focused primarily on traditions practiced by homogeneous, rural groups living in relative isolation from other groups. Today, however, folk culture is more inclusively recognized as a dynamic representation of both modern and rural constituents.

Related to the cultivation of community and group identity, folk culture is quite often imbued with a sense of place. If elements of a folk culture are copied by, or moved to, a foreign locale, they will still carry strong connotations of their original place of creation.

7.2 Folk Culture in China and the West

7.2.1 Folk Culture in China

China is comprised of 56 ethnic groups and nearly each of them has its own fantastic and time-honored folk culture. Chinese folk music, folk dancing, folk rituals, folk beliefs, folk festivals, folk operas, folk myths, folk epics, folk legends, folk art, and folk architecture and so on are breathtakingly amazing. However, the systematical investigation, catalogue, restoration, protection and research are still unavailable. A multitude of domestic scholars have been calling on the attention of governments and non-governmental organs at all levels to make up for the defects in protecting, publicizing and cultivating folk cultures.

Splendid Chinese culture consists of elite culture, classical culture (traditional or ancient culture) and folk culture. The three portions of Chinese culture are equally important and irreplaceable respectively. Particularly, the folk culture should be further protected. It is created by hands and hearts of people. Over the past 5,000 years, it has been largely collected and closely related to commoners' life and affections. Generally, our national tradition of ideological system is preserved in Chinese elite and classic culture, while national affection and individuality are vividly taken on by Chinese folk culture.

For example, to many Chinese people today, the Spring Festival begins on the last day of the last lunar month, however, traditionally, this starts on the La Ba Festival or Twenty-third Day of the last lunar month and ends in the Lantern Festival on the fifteenth day of the first month. The climax of the festive celebration is on the Chinese New Year's Eve and the New Year's Day. The legend of New Year goes that in ancient times a beast called *nian* often attacked house animals in warm seasons, and in the cold winter it would eat humans when the food resources were scarce. People were living in ultimate fear because they had to fight with it all the time. Finally, they discovered the beast *nian* was afraid of three things: red color, fire light and loud sound. Therefore, one night in winter people had to hang red colored wooden boards on their houses' door frames, made bonfire outside the door, and hit gongs and drums all night long. The beast was scared, not entering the village and staying in its mountain den. The following day people celebrated their victory over the wild beast and a banquet was held. This tradition is still followed today by the Chinese in most areas as a New Year celebration, to which the night is the New Year's Eve, and the New Year's Day follows.

The Lantern Festival falls on the 15th day of the first lunar month, usually in February or March in the solar calendar. As early as the Western Han Dynasty (202 BC—AD 9), it had become a festival with great significance. Lanterns of various shapes and sizes are hung in the streets, attracting countless visitors. Children will hold self-made or bought lanterns to stroll with on the streets, extremely excited. It is also a time to eat glutinous rice dumplings which symbolize family unity.

Qingming Festival is one of the 24 seasonal division points in China, after which the temperature will rise up and rainfall increases. It is a festival of commemoration combining sadness and happiness. People visit the gravesites of their ancestors to pay respects to the dead at their tombs and hold memorial ceremonies in honor of their ancestors. It is also a day to celebrate the coming of spring with outdoor activities such as picnicking, tug-of-war, kite-flying, swinging, dancing, etc.

The Dragon Boat Festival falls on the 5th day of the 5th lunar month. It has had a history of more than 2,000 years. The best-known story of its origin centers on a great patriotic poet named Qu Yuan. People have Dragon Boat Races, eat zongzi (dumpling made of glutinous rice wrapped in bamboo or reed leaves), drink realgar wine, and carry a spice bag around with them.

The Double Seventh Festival, on the 7th day of the 7th lunar month, is a traditional festival full of romance, according to which the Cowherd Man and the Weaving Maid will meet on a bridge of magpies on the sky across the Milky Way once a year.

Apart from festivals, Chinese food is an important part of Chinese folk culture, which includes foods originating from the diverse regions of China, as well as from Chinese people in other parts of the world.

The preference for seasoning and cooking techniques in different provinces depends on historical background and ethnic groups. Geographic features including mountains, rivers, forests and deserts also have a strong effect on the local available ingredients and cooking techniques, for example, residents in the provinces of Hunan and Sichuan are especially crazy for spicy food due to the wet weather related to their locations to the south of the Yangtse River.

The most praised traditional *Four Major Cuisines* are Chuan, Lu, Yue and Huaiyang, representing West, North, South and East China cuisine correspondingly. Modern *Eight Cuisines* of China are Anhui, Guangdong, Fujian, Hunan, Jiangsu, Shandong, Sichuan, and Zhejiang cuisines.

Color, smell and taste are the three traditional aspects to describe Chinese food. Its meaning, shape and nutrition related to ingredients, cuttings, cooking time and seasoning are stressed, especially to those who are better educated.

7.2.2 Folk Culture in the West

Folk culture in the west is equally rich in diversity, but it will suffice to mention a few as examples.

Christmas or Christmas Day is an annual festival commemorating the birth of Jesus Christ, observed most commonly on December 25 as a religious and cultural celebration among billions of people around the world. Christmas Day is a public holiday in many of the world's nations, and is an integral part of the holiday season.

Christians celebrate Christmas in various ways. In addition to the attendance of church services, there are other devotions and traditions. A long artistic tradition is producing painted depictions of the nativity. Nativity scenes are traditionally set in a stable with livestock and include Mary, Joseph, the infant Jesus in the manger, the three wise men, the shepherds and their sheep, the angels, and the Star of Bethlehem.

Thanksgiving Day is a national holiday celebrated in Canada, in the United States, in some of the Caribbean islands and in Liberia. It began as a day of giving thanks for the blessing of the harvest and of the preceding year. Thanksgiving is celebrated on the second Monday of October in Canada and on the fourth Thursday of November in the United States, and around the same part of the year in other places. Although Thanksgiving has historical roots in religious and cultural traditions, it has long been celebrated as a secular holiday as well.

Prayers of thanks and special thanksgiving ceremonies are common among almost all religions after harvests and at other times. The Thanksgiving holiday's history in North

America is rooted in English traditions dating from the Protestant Reformation. It also has aspects of a harvest festival, even though the harvest in New England occurs well before the late-November date on which the modern Thanksgiving holiday is celebrated.

A pow wow (also powwow or pow-wow) is a social gathering held by many different Native American communities. The word derives from the Narragansett word powwaw, meaning "spiritual leader". A similar gathering by California Native Peoples usually in the fall is called a Big Time. A modern pow wow is a specific type of event for Native American people to meet and dance, sing, socialize, and honor their cultures. Pow wows may be private or public. There is generally a dancing competition, often with significant prize money awarded. Pow wows vary in length from a one-day event, to major pow wows called for a special occasion which can be up to one week long.

Planning for a pow wow generally begins months, perhaps even a year, in advance of the event by a group of people usually referred to as a pow wow committee. Pow wows may be sponsored by a tribal organization, by an American Native community within an urban area, a Native American Studies program or American Native club on a college or university campus, tribe, or any other organization that can provide startup funds, insurance, and volunteer workers.

Music for pow wow dance competition and other activities is provided by a "Drum", a group of performers who play a large, specially designed drum and sing traditional songs. The number of members of a drum group may vary, but is usually at least four people, and can be far more. Some members of the drum group may wear traditional regalia and dance as well as drum, other times drummers simply wear street clothing. Drums usually rotate the duty of providing songs for the dancers, each taking a turn at the direction of the pow wow management.

7.3 Chinese-English Translation Texts in the Field of Folk Culture

7.3.1 Cultural Supplementation of Source-Specific Concepts

Cultural supplementation means adding the cultural background which is very familiar for source language readers and therefore taken for granted, but readers of the target language will feel at a loss for the missing cultural background, so it is the translator's job to make up for the default information.

When 元宵 was mentioned in a *China Daily* paper, the writer added the following cultural information:

The lantern festival, which falls on February 26 this year, is the 15th day of the first month of the lunar calendar. The festival traditionally features big fireworks display, mass performance of *yangkou*(秧歌) folk dances, land boat, stilt walking, lion dances and dragon dances. Other main activities are to appreciate the bright nightscape highlighted by colored lanterns, or to enjoy yuan xiao or glutinous flout balls with sweet or meat fillings.

In translating the names of dishes (i. e. Chinese food contained in dishes), also, much information must be augmented to make the food understandable.

Examples can be found in the following correspondences:

全家福: stewed (炖) assorted meat

玉扳禅师: stewed potatoes with mushrooms

佛跳墙: Buddha jumps over the wall (Steamed abalone with shark's fin and fish maw).

馄饨: a kind of dumpling made with thin wrappers, usu. served in soup

Also, many names other than those for food are hardly understandable:

旗袍: a close-fitting woman's dress with high neck and slit skirt

太极拳: school of popular traditional martial art marked for slow and graceful movements that are designed to attack or counterattack, keep fit, prevent and treat diseases

If they are respectively translated into *a kind of gown worn by Chinese women* and *shadow boxing*, they are still not informative enough, so a more detailed introduction as above is required.

7.3.2 Retaining the Cultural Connotations of Source Proverbs and Folklores

Chinese and English each has its own proverbs and folklores, some of which may happen to be very close in content or plot, so translators have to be very prudent in bringing them together as one translating another, because they will differ in one way or another.

For instance, a Chinese proverb says 有钱能使鬼推磨, which is a little bit equivalent to *money can make the mare go*, but the cultural connotation is totally lost in this ready correspondence. *Money makes the devil turn your mill*, on the contrary, carries with it a rich load of cultural connotation.

Slang words or local sayings should be handled with great care:

二百五: blockhead (木头人) or dumbbell (蠢人)

小菜一碟: a piece of cake

歇个脚: to get a load off one's feet

没招了: to be at the end of one's tether

Folklores have experienced a long period of social development and have accumulated a rich association, the episodes cannot be simplied or deleted. In《梁山伯与祝英台》, the heroine Zhu Yingtai suggested that she (in the guise of a boy) and Liang Shanbo become sworn brothers:

为兄弟两人立刻写好名帖，盟誓他俩应像亲兄弟那样互相忠贞不渝，山伯一九岁为兄，英台一七为弟，银心在香炉上点好了香放在地上，目睹两人换帖成为结拜兄弟。

It was Yingtai's sudden suggestion that they should become sworn brothers then and there, the two wrote out name cards at once, testifying their faithfulness to each other as blood brothers. Liang Shanbo aged 19, was elder brother, Zhu Yingtai aged 17, younger brother. Yinxin lighted joss sticks in the incense burner place on the ground, witnessing the two become sworn brothers as they exchange the cards.

The underlined parts are rich with Chinese cultural connotations and must be carefully considered.

7.4 Samples

The first sample is drawn from the folklore *Liang Shanbo and Zhu Yingtai*(《梁山伯与祝英台》)：

从前有个姓祝的地主，人称祝员外，他的女儿祝英台不仅美丽大方，而且非常的聪明好学。但由于古时候女子不能进学堂读书，祝英台只好日日倚在窗栏上，望着大街上身背着书箱来来往往的读书人，心里羡慕极了！难道女子只能在家里绣花吗？为什么我不能去上学？

Long long ago there was a landlord surnamed Zhu. He had a daughter named Zhu Yingtai who was very beautiful and smart and liked learning very much. However, girls were not permitted to go to school in that old time. So she had to stay at home and looked at the students coming and going on the street through the window every day. She envied them very much and thought: Why do girls have to stay at home and do the embroidering? Why can't I go to school?

她突然反问自己：对啊！我为什么就不能上学呢？想到这儿，祝英台赶紧回到房间，鼓起勇气向父母要求："爹，娘，我要到杭州去读书。我可以穿男人的衣服，扮成男人的样子，一定不让别人认出来，你们就答应我吧！"祝员外夫妇开始不同意，但经不住英台撒娇哀求，只好答应了。

Suddenly she asked herself, "Why can't I go to school?" So she went back to the room and asked her parents with courage, "Dad, Mum, I want to go to Hangzhou to attend school. I can wear man's garments and act like a man, so that I will not be recognized. I promise. Please do let me go, please!" The old couple didn't agree at first, but had to give in later because Yingtai implored continually.

第二天一清早，天刚蒙蒙亮，祝英台就和丫鬟扮成男装，辞别父母，带着书箱，兴高采烈地出发去杭州了。到了学堂，祝英台遇见了一个叫梁山伯的男同学，学问出众，人品也十分优秀。两人一见如故，常常在一起谈古论今，吟诗诵文。后来，两人结拜为兄弟，更是时时刻刻，形影不离。

The next morning, Yingtai and her maid, both in man's suits, set out to Hangzhou happily after bidding farewell to her parents. At school she met a classmate named Liang Shanbo who was excellent and knowledgeable. They felt like old friends the moment they saw each other. The two talked and discussed together a lot from then on. Later, they decided to be sworn brothers and became more intimate than before.

春去秋来，一晃三年过去了，学年期满，该是打点行装、拜别老师、返回家乡的时候了。同窗共烛整三载，祝英台已经深深爱上了她的梁兄，而梁山伯虽不知祝英台是女生，但对她也恋恋不舍。回到家后，都日夜思念着对方。

Three years soon went past. It was time to say goodbye to her teacher and return home. Zhu Yingtai felt she was deeply in love with Liang Shanbo after three years' studying together. Liang also hated to see her going home although he didn't know that she was a girl actually. They missed each other day and night after their parting.

几个月后，梁山伯前往祝家拜访，结果令他又惊又喜。原来这时，他见到的祝英台，已不再是那个清秀的小书生，而是一位年轻美貌的大姑娘。再见的那一刻，他们都明白了彼此之间的感情，早已是心心相印。此后，梁山伯请人到祝家去求亲。可祝员外早已把女儿许配给了有钱人家的少爷马公子。梁山伯顿觉万念俱灰，一病不起，没多久就死去了。听到梁山伯去世的消息，一直在与父母抗争的祝英台反而突然变得异常镇静。她套上红衣红裙，走进了迎亲的花轿。

Several months later, Liang Shanbo went to visit Zhu Yingtai and found with surprise and joy that Yingtai was a girl. Later, Liang Shanbo sent a matchmaker to the Zhu's to get the permission of marrying Yingtai. But the landlord had already accepted the proposal of a young master surnamed Ma, son of a rich family. Liang Shanbo felt utterly sad and got severely sick. Soon he died. Yingtai who opposed her father's decision of marrying Ma became strangely calm when she learned of Liang's death. She put on the red wedding apparel and went into the bride sedan.

路过梁山伯的坟前时，忽然间飞沙走石，花轿不得不停了下来。只见祝英台走出轿来，脱去红装，一身素服，缓缓地走到坟前，跪下来放声大哭，霎时间风雨飘摇，雷声大作，"轰"的一声，坟墓裂开了，祝英台似乎又见到了她的梁兄那温柔的面庞，她微笑着纵身跳了进去。接着又是一声巨响，坟墓合上了。这时风消云散，雨过天晴，各种野花在风中轻柔地摇曳，一对美丽的蝴蝶从坟头飞出来，在阳光下自由地翩翩起舞。

When the party escorting the bride passed by the tomb of Liang Shanbo, wind blew hard out of expectation. The party had to stop for the time being. Yingtai came out from the sedan and took off the red wedding costume and was in mourning white. She cried loudly and sadly in front of the tomb. A sudden thunder-storm came and the tomb split with a loud noise. Yingtai, who loved Liang deeply, jumped into the tomb with a smile before the others could realize it. Then the tomb closed with a loud noise again. The wind ceased and the cloud scattered. Flowers were dancing in the breeze. Two beautiful butterflies flew out of the tomb and danced elegantly, freely and happily in the sun.

The second sample is drawn from Huangmei Drama *Female Prince Consort* (《女驸马》):

为救李郎离家园
To save Li Zhaoting, I left my home
谁料皇榜中状元
Who would have thought I'll score as top scholar
中状元着红袍
As top scholar, I wear the red gown
帽插宫花好啊好新鲜
Flowers of honor on my hat, a very fresh experience for me
我也曾赴过琼林宴
I have already been to the banquet in the Jade Forest
我也曾打马御街前
Paraded on horseback on the Imperial Street
人人夸我潘安貌
Everyone praises me for my good look
原来纱帽罩啊罩婵娟
But this official's hat actually covers a beautiful lady
我考状元不为把名显
I didn't take the exams for reputation
我考状元不为作高官
I didn't take the exam for becoming a high official
为了多情的李公子
But for my much beloved Li Zhaoting
夫妻恩爱花好月儿圆
For the perfect happiness of man and wife in conjugal love
...

7.5 A Glossary of Folk Culture in English and Chinese

八卦炉 eight trigrams furnace

八仙 the Eight Immortals

弼马温 the protector of the horses
财神爷 the God of Wealth
长生殿 Palace of Eternal Life
赤脚大仙 Barefoot Immortal
二郎真君 True Lord Erlang
蟠桃园 the Immortality Peach Garden
花果山 Mountain of Flowers and Fruits
金箍棒 golden cudgel
雷公 the Thunder God
灵霄宝殿 Hall of Miraculous Mist
龙王 Dragon King
炉火神 the Fire God
吕洞宾 Lu Dongbin
罗汉 arhat
美猴王 Handsome Monkey King
门神 Door Gods
七十二般变化 seventy-two different forms
齐天大圣 the Great Sage Equalling Heaven
塞翁失马,焉知非福 Misfortune may be an actual blessing.
杀鸡用牛刀 break a butterfly on the wheel
世外桃源 a fictitious land of peace away from the turmoil of the world
水帘洞 Water Curtain Cave
四大天王 Four Heavenly Kings
太白金星 Great White Planet
太上老君 Lord Lao Zi of the Great Monad
托塔李天王 Heavenly King with a Pagoda in Hand
王母娘娘 the Queen Mother of the West
五行山 Five Elements Mountain
阎王爷 King of Hell
瑶池 Jade Pool
玉皇大帝 the Jade Emperor
灶王爷 the Kitchen God

《霸王别姬》Farewell to My Concubine
《春江花月夜》Moon and Flower in the Spring River
《封神榜》Granting Titles to Gods
《贵妃醉酒》Drunkened Concubine
《荒山泪》Tears of Huangshan

《将相和》General and Premier Make Up
《借东风》East Wind
《梁祝》(小提琴协奏曲) Butterfly Love
《林家铺子》The Shop of Lin Family
《龙须沟》Longxu Ditch
《牡丹亭》Peony Pavilion
《拍案惊奇》Surprise Stories to Make One Slap the Desk
《琵琶记》The Story of Pipa
《清明上河图》Riverside Scene at Qingming Festival
《群英会》Gathering of Heroes
《十面埋伏》(古曲) Ambush from All Sides
《桃花扇》The Peach Blossom Fan
《天仙配》Goddess Marriage
《杨门女将》Women General of Yang Family

Chapter 8 Contrast of Sino-Western Cultures and Chinese-English Translation Texts in the Field of Catch Phrase

8.1 What Is Catch Phrase

A catch phrase (or catchphrase) is a phrase or expression recognized by its repeated utterance. Such phrases often originate in pop culture and in cyber space, and typically spread through a variety of mass media (such as literature and publishing, motion pictures, television and radio), as well as word of mouth. Some become the de facto or literal "trademark" or "signature" of the person or character with whom they originated, and can be instrumental in the typecasting (beneficially or otherwise) of a particular actor.

8.2 Cultural Contrast of the Chinese Language and the English Language

8.2.1 The Chinese Language

The Chinese language is a group of related but in many cases mutually unintelligible language varieties, forming a branch of the Sino-Tibetan language family. Chinese is spoken by the Han ethnic group and 55 minor ethnic groups in China. Nearly 1.2 billion people speak some form of the Chinese as their first language.

The varieties of Chinese are usually described by native speakers as dialects of a single Chinese language, but linguists note that they are as diverse as a language family. The internal diversity of Chinese has been likened to that of the Romance languages, but may be even more varied. There are between 7 and 13 main regional groups of Chinese (depending on classification scheme), of which the most spoken by far is Mandarin (about 960 million), followed by Wu (80 million), Yue (60 million) and Min (70 million). Most of these groups are mutually unintelligible, although some, like Xiang and the Southwest Mandarin dialects, may share a vocabulary and some degree of intelligibility. All varieties of Chinese are tonal and analytic.

Standard Chinese (Putonghua) is a standardized form of spoken Chinese based on the Beijing dialect of Mandarin. It is the official language of China, as well as one of four official languages of Singapore. It is one of the six official languages of the United Nations. The written form of the standard language, based on the logograms known as Chinese characters, is shared by literate speakers of otherwise unintelligible dialects.

Chinese can be traced back to a hypothetical Sino-Tibetan proto-language. The first written records appeared over 3,000 years ago. As the language evolved over this period, the various local varieties became mutually unintelligible. In reaction, central governments repeatedly sought to promulgate a unified standard.

Until the mid-20th century, most of the Chinese people living in many parts of southern China spoke only their local language. As a practical measure, officials of the Ming and Qing dynasties carried out the administration of the empire using a common language based on Mandarin varieties, known as Guānhuà (官话). For most of this period, this language was a variant based on the dialect spoken in the Nanjing area, though not identical to any single dialect. By the middle of the 19th century, the Beijing dialect had become dominant and was essential for any business with the imperial court.

The people's Republic of China founded in 1949 retained this standard, calling it pǔtōnghuà (普通话). The national language is now used in education, mass media, and other formal situations in China.

8.2.2 The English Language

The English language is a West Germanic language that was first spoken in early medieval England and is now a global lingua franca. It is an official language of almost 60 sovereign states, the most commonly spoken language in the United Kingdom, the United States, Canada, Australia, Ireland, and New Zealand, and a widely spoken language in countries in the Caribbean, Africa, and South Asia. It is the third most common native language in the world, after Mandarin and Spanish. It is the most widely learned second language and is an official language of the United Nations, of the European Union, and of many other world and regional international organisations.

English has developed over the course of more than 1,400 years. The earliest forms of English, a set of Anglo-Frisian dialects brought to Great Britain by Anglo-Saxon settlers in the fifth century, are called Old English. Middle English began in the late 11th century with the Norman conquest of England. Early Modern English began in the late 15th century with the introduction of the printing press to London and the *King James Bible* as well as the Great Vowel Shift. Through the worldwide influence of the British Empire, modern English spread around the world from the 17th to mid-20th centuries. Through all types of printed and electronic media, as well as the emergence of the United States as a global superpower, English has become the leading language of international discourse and the lingua franca in many regions and in professional contexts such as science, navigation, and law.

English began to rise in prestige during the reign of Henry V. Around 1430, the Court of Chancery in Westminster began using English in its official documents, and a new standard form of Middle English, known as Chancery Standard, developed from the dialects of London and the East Midlands. In 1476, William Caxton introduced the printing press to England and began publishing the first printed books in London, expanding the influence of this form of English. Literature from the Early Modern period includes the works of William Shakespeare and the translation of the *Bible* commissioned by King James I. By the late 18th century, the British Empire had facilitated the spread of English through its colonies and geopolitical dominance. Commerce, science and technology, diplomacy, art, and formal education all contributed to English becoming the first truly global language. English also facilitated worldwide international communication. As England continued to form new colonies, these in turn became independent and developed their own norms for how to speak and write the language. English was adopted in North America, India, parts of Africa, Australia, and many other regions. In the post-colonial period, some of the newly created nations that had multiple indigenous languages opted to continue using English as the official language to avoid the political difficulties inherent in promoting any one indigenous language above the others. In the 20th century the growing economic and cultural influence of the United States and its status as a superpower following the Second World War has, along with worldwide broadcasting in English by the BBC and other broadcasters, significantly accelerated the spread of the language across the planet. By the 21st century, English was more widely spoken and written than any language has ever been.

8.3 Chinese-English Translation Texts in the Field of Catch Phrase

Translation in the field of catch phrase is somewhat deviating in the two sections coming up below because catch words are culture-specific and language-specific. It is not likely that catch words in one language will develop along the same path as those in another language, so interlanguage contrast of catch words will give way to intralanguage contrast, but of course how they are translated into the other language remains part of our focus.

8.3.1 Existing Words Obtaining New Meanings

囧 is one of the most popularly used catch words in recent years in the Chinese society. It is not newly invented, but an archaic word which has been refound and given new life to. Originally it meant *brightness*, now conveys the meaning of *embarrassment*, *anxiety*, *worry*, *sadness*, *depressed*, *dumbness*, *dumbfoundedness* or the like.

山寨 literally means *a mountain fortress* or *a bandit stronghold in the mountain*, figuratively means *rip-off products* or *copycatting*.

雷 means *thunder*, a noun, but, as a catch word, it is used as a verb as in 雷人 and 雷倒 etc. to denote *surprise*, *shock*, *astonishment* or *absurdity*.

打酱油 literally means to buy soy sauce, figuratively means *to play a trivial or unimportant role*, or *it's none of my business*. Its new meaning is derived from a true story: Once a person in Guangzhou was asked to give his opinion of a certain sex scandal, the man answered, "It is none of my business. I am just out to get some soy sauce."

8.3.2 Innovation of New Expressions

The previous section talks of existing words used as catch words, so in this section it is due turn to come to the innotation of new expressions used as catch words.

菜(鸟) literally is the collocation of vegetable + bird, which means a green hand, novice or beginner. An example:

我是菜鸟,还靠你当师傅带带哦。

I'm still a green hand while you are an old hand and I need your help.

人肉搜索, literally *human flesh search*, means *mass-sourced man-hunting* or *cyber man-hunting*.

给力 is used as an adjective, so a new word *geilivable* is coined for its correspondance. It means *strong*, *powerful*, *cool*, *awesome*, etc.

凤凰男与孔雀女: Phoenix man (a man who grew up poor or in the countryside, but after many years of hard work moved to a big city and married a city girl) and Peacock woman (a city girl who grew up in a well-off family, spoiled by her parents, knowing nothing about the hardship of life)

经济适用男: a budget husband (Although not earning a lot, the budget husbands don't have bad habits such as drinking, smoking or gambling and are family-oriented. They are regarded as the first choice for husband by present office ladies.)

哥吃的不是面,是寂寞: What I am eating is not noodles but loneliness. A liberal translation can be *my loneliness is killing me*!

这事儿不能说太细: This cannot be told in details.

This is the reply made by an official when interviewed by a reporter on a TV program about a very sensitive political issue. Later on this statement represents the excuse used to reject inquiries on issues of public concern and is synonymous with official evasion of public scrutiny.

被 is a passive voice marker, the verb it introduces is normally transitive, but as a catch word, its extended meaning of *being forced to do something* or *being unwilling to do something* comes from its collocation with an intransitive verb as in 被就业, 被自杀, 被增长, etc., often translated into *be said/presumed/announced/reported to do...* Sometimes they are equivalent to *be done by others* as *be suicided by others*. What the relevant reality is faked-up. 被 can function as a modifier as in *faked-up employment* or *faked-up increase*.

8.4 Samples

Below are a few catch phrases used by native speakers of English in their everyday talk.

I don't want to be the third wheel.
我不想当电灯泡。

I am the one-woman kinda man/woman.
我是那种从一而终的男人/女人。

Those boys like to hit on me all the time.
那些男生老爱找我搭讪。

You should have chivalry.
你应该有点绅士风度。

I saw you smooching that girl just outside my window.
我看到你在我的窗外亲那个女孩喔。

I'm all over you.
我对你非常着迷。

I'm over you.
我跟你之间完了。

Are you trying to seduce me?
你想要勾引我吗?

What is the fuss?
吵什么?

Nothing tricky.
别耍花招。

It can be a killer.
这是个伤脑筋的问题。

The following are catch phrases used by Chinese native speakers in their everyday speech.

下海 jumping into the sea

Jumping into the sea was often used to refer to the phenomenon of people breaking away from the constraints of a planned economy system to embrace the market economy.

下岗再就业 be laid off and get re-employed

Being *laid off* was never heard before the State Council made the decision to reform the country's state-owned enterprises in 1986. Thus, workers in such enterprises boasted of a lifelong job or "iron rice bowl". To adapt to the market economy and improve the competitiveness of state-owned enterprises in the 1990s, China began restructuring its enterprises by laying off some staff members and encouraging them to get re-employed.

农民工 migrant worker

Reforms in rural areas, with collectively owned farmland contracted to individual families, freed about 100 million peasants from farm work. A policy change in 1984 allowed them to find jobs in cities. After China decided to move to a market economy in 1992, the massive migration of rural laborers started.

上网 surfing the Internet

The Internet was introduced in China early in the 1990s. It quickly gained popularity and made a huge impact on society. While online music, instant communication services, video streaming and online games entertained millions of Chinese, the Internet also became a powerful news medium where information was disclosed, shared and publicized quickly.

雄起 Go! Go!

The phrase is a dialect of Sichuan province. It was originally used in the 1990s by soccer fans to cheer their favorite teams. The phrase was later used widely outside sports to encourage people to keep up their spirits in gloomy times. After the May 12 earthquake in Sichuan in 2008, the Chinese used the phrase to show their care and support for quake-hit areas and people.

8.5 A Glossary of Catch Phrases in English and Chinese

悲催 a tear-inducing misery

北约、华约 Peking University-led enrollment alliance; Tsinghua University-led enrollment alliance

搏出位 be a famewhore; seek attention
穿越剧 time-travel TV drama
淡定 calm; unruffled
范儿 style
富二代 rich second generation
腹黑 scheming
哥只是传说 Brother is only a legend.
海归(海龟) overseas returnee
纠结 ambivalent
坑爹 the reverse of one's expectation
林来疯 Linsanity
萝莉 Lolita
卖萌 act cute
秒杀 seckill; speed kill
你懂的 It goes without saying that...
拼爹 daddy-is-the-key; parents privilege competition
人肉搜索 human flesh search engine
山寨 fake, counterfeit, copycat
伤不起 vulnerable; be prone to getting hurt
神马都是浮云 It's all fleeting cloud.
剩女 leftover ladies; 3S women (3S=single, seventies, stuck)
忐忑 anxious
吐槽 disclose one's secret
团购 group purchasing
微博 Microblog
蜗居 dwelling narrowness; a bedsitter
犀利哥 Brother Sharp
羡慕嫉妒恨 envious, jealous and hateful
小清新 like a breath of fresh air
蚁族 ant-like graduates
宅男 Otaku ("homebody" in English); geek
折翼的天使 an angel with broken wings
至于你信不信,反正我是信了 Whether you believe it or not, I am convinced.
自主招生 university autonomous enrollment
做人呢,最重要是开心 Happiness is the way.

Chapter 9 Contrast of Sino-Western Cultures and Chinese-English Translation Texts in the Field of Sport

9.1 What Is Sport

Sport (UK) or sports (US) are all forms of usually competitive physical activity or games which, through casual or organised participation, aim to use, maintain or improve physical ability and skills while providing entertainment to participants, and in some cases, spectators.

Sport is generally recognised as activities which are based on physical athleticism or physical dexterity, with the largest major competitions such as the Olympic Games admitting only sports meeting this definition, and other organisations such as the Council of Europe using definitions precluding activities without a physical element from classification as sports. However, a number of competitive, but non-physical, activities claim recognition as mind sports.

9.2 Cultural Contrast of Sport in China and the West

9.2.1 Sport in China

China has a variety of competitive sports. Traditional Chinese culture regards physical fitness as an important characteristic. China has its own national quadrennial multi-sport event similar to the Olympic Games called the National Games.

The influx of modern sports appeared in China since the beginning of the 20th century. The People's Republic of China emphasizes sports and the government funds and trains talented young people into professional players, especially beginning in the mid-20th century.

Ping pong is one of the biggest amateur recreational sports with an estimated 200 million players. Badminton is also well established and popular.

Boxing in China began as a street sport in the 1920s, mainly in the port cities of Shanghai and Guangzhou, where foreign sailors were pitted against local fighters in the ring. The sport grew rapidly and unsupervised by the Chinese government. Chinese boxing style is similar to Western boxing style, with influences from traditional Chinese martial arts.

Dragon boat racing dates back about 2,000 years ago and remains a traditional event held around China every year. There is evidence that Cuju, a sport similar to football, was played in China during the 2nd and 3rd centuries BC. From the Song Dynasty on Taijiquan and similar qigong martial arts activities became popular in China.

China led the gold medal count (51) at the 2008 Summer Olympics in Beijing and hosted the 2014 Youth Olympic Games from August 16 to 28, 2014 in Nanjing. Beijing is also expecting to host the 2022 Winter Olympics.

9.2.2 Sport in the West

The United Kingdom has given birth to a range of major international sports including: association football, rugby, darts, cricket, golf, tennis, table tennis, badminton, squash, rounders, hockey, boxing, snooker, billiards, curling and even baseball.

Football is the most popular sport and is played from August to May. Rugby League is traditionally a winter sport, but since the late 1990s the elite competition has been played in the summer to minimize competition for attention with football. Rugby Union is also a winter sport. Cricket is played in summer, from April to September. There is also a professional Ice Hockey league operating in Great Britain called the Elite Ice Hockey League.

The modern global game of football evolved out of traditional football games played in England in the 19th century and today is the highest profile sport in England and Scotland by a very wide margin. This has been the case for generations, but the gap is widely perceived to have increased since the early 1990s, and football's dominance is often seen as a threat to other sports. Football is also very popular in Wales and Northern Ireland, though Rugby Union and Gaelic Games respectively attract much larger crowds and television audiences.

Sports in the United States are an important part of the country's culture. The four major professional sports leagues in the United States are Major League Baseball (MLB), the National Basketball Association (NBA), the National Football League (NFL), and the National Hockey League (NHL).

Sports are particularly associated with education in the United States, with most high schools and universities having organized sports. College sports competitions play an important role in the American sporting culture, and college football and college basketball are as popular as professional sports in some parts of the country. The major sanctioning body for college sports is the National Collegiate Athletic Association (NCAA).

The United States Olympic Committee (USOC) is the National Olympic Committee for the United States. American athletes have won a total of 2,570 medals in Summer Olympic Games and another 253 in Winter Olympic Games. American athletes have won more medals in athletics (track and field) (738, 29%) and swimming (489, 19%) than any other nation.

9.3 Chinese-English Translation Texts in the Field of Sport

9.3.1 Restoring the Dropped-out Information and Understanding the Initialisms

In sports match reports, many words are dropped out to save space. So in translation the dropped-out words or implicitly-stated playing rules have to be restored to make the report understandable to the target language readers.

For instance, in a golf match in the United States, as in (1), *Congressional* stands for *Congressional Country Club*. *Under par* means fewer than the standard number of shots, the standard is 71 shots. The fewer shots you need, the more you score. Only when the translator gets familiar with the playing rules, can she figure out the number of 16 shots, 3 shots and 1 shot.

(1) Rory Mcllroy, the 22-year-old, broke a host of scoring records and shot a final-round 69 to end 16 under par at Congressional. Australian Jason Day (68) was second, with Lee Westwood (70) tied in third. Rory led from start to finish, carding 65, 66, 68, 69 to post a tournament record total of 268, four better than the previous mark.

22 岁的罗里·麦克罗伊在美国高尔夫公开赛决赛中打出 69 杆,以总杆低于标准杆 16 杆的破纪录成绩获得冠军。澳大利亚选手简森·戴伊 68 杆,以低于标准杆 3 杆的成绩,获得亚军。英格兰选手李·维斯特伍德打出 70 杆,以低于标准杆 1 杆的成绩,获得第三名。罗里从一开始就遥遥领先,四轮比赛的得分分别是 65, 66, 68, 69,总杆 268 杆,比上次比赛低 4 杆。

In the field of sport or sports match, many initialisms may become obstacles for the translator. Translators are supposed to know the frequently used intitialisms or at least know where to find their meanings. Here are some examples:

IOC (International Olympic Committee):国际奥委会(国际奥林匹克委员会)

IAAF (International Association of Athletics Federations):国际田联(国际田径联合会)

FIFA (Federation Internationale de Football Association):国际足联(国际足球联合会)

9.3.2 Paying Special Attention to Technical Terminologies

Sport texts are heavily imbued with technical terms of all sorts, negligence of which will bring about a ridiculous effect in translation. So special attention should be paid to the rendering of technical terminologies as follows:

play-off: 季后赛

butterfly stroke: 蝶泳

all-stars game: 全明星赛

Technical terms do not always present themselves as a one-to-one correspondence from the source to the target, as an interesting contrast, the equivalent in the other language may depend upon the context in which it occurs, for example, the English counterpart for 运动员 varies from context to context:

击剑运动员 fencer

跳水运动员 diver

摔跤运动员 wrestler

体操运动员 gymnast

Similarly, 裁判 may have different sayings in English depending on which specific game is involved:

田径裁判 judge

足球裁判 referee

乒乓球/羽毛球裁判 umpire

9.3.3 Translation of Rhetorical Devices and Cultural Images

Rhetorical devices abound in both English and Chinese. Sometimes they correspond, sometimes they do not.

(2) Rocket Roars to the 17th Consecutive Victory

火箭队豪气冲天,取得 17 连胜的惊人成绩

In (2), the use of *roar* is a pun, on the one hand rockets as space vehicles will roar into the outer space, on the other hand it says of the basketball team Rocket which did a good job in a match. But in the Chinese version, the pun breaks down: its two senses are independently represented by 豪气冲天 and 取得.

(3) Japan beat Sweden 3-1 thanks to a double from Nahomi Kawasumi, including a spectacular 35-metre lob(高球).

日本凭川澄奈穗美个人梅开二度,最终以 3:1 淘汰瑞典,跻身决赛。包括一记漂亮的 35 米远距离吊射。

In (3) the word *double* is rendered into a metaphorical image 梅开二度. 梅(plum bloom) is a good image, referring to success or victory. *Bloom for a second time* metaphorically stands for a second success.

Cultural images are greatly emphasized in Chinese, because they can add to the aesthetic effect of a writing. But in English many have to be removed, as in (4), or else explained in due detail, as in (5) and (6).

(4) 形意拳：此拳以五行生克、阴阳变化为原理，内存于心，外显于形。取之于各种动物之形神势貌，故名为形意。

Xingyiquan: This boxing, based on the wuxing and yin/yang theory, stresses both the internal force and the external form. During the performance, the player imitates the movements of various animals. That is why it is called Xingyiquan, the Imitation Boxing.

(5) 有内三合、外三合之六合法要，有臂拳、崩拳、钻拳、炮拳、横拳五个基本拳法。演练起来劲沉力脆，刚柔相济，虎虎生风。

Intrinsic to this boxing are six integrations, of which the internal three are integrations of mind and intention, intention and energy, energy and force while the external three actually refer to coordinated actions of shoulders and thighs, elbows and knees, hands and feet. The boxing comprises five basic moves: chopping, crushing, drilling, exploding and crossing. Throughout the performance, harmony can be sensed between force, grace, vigor and speed.

(6) 日月追风刀：此刀法轻如燕、稳如山、快如风，有技击、观赏之价值。

The Windstorm Falchion: This falchion can be played as lightly as a dancing swallow, as firmly as a towering mountain, and as fast as windstorm. It is fine for either aesthetical appreciation or practical fighting.

There are many cultural images in the above example, such as 五行 and 阴阳; metaphorical images such as 轻如燕，稳如山，快如风 and 演练起来劲沉力脆，刚柔相济，虎虎生风.

In translation, sometimes literal translation will do, such as 轻如燕，稳如山，快如风 translated into *as lightly as a dancing swallow, as firmly as a towering mountain, and as fast as windstorm*. Sometimes the translator should be considerate enough to add some extra information to facilitate the understanding of the target language readers, so the underlined part is added: of which the internal three are integrations of mind and intention, intention and energy, energy and force while the external three actually refer to coordinated actions of shoulders and thighs, elbows and knees, hands and feet.

9.4 Sample

Football Fix 5-a-side Rules (Excerpt)

《五人制足球竞赛规则》(节选)

A match is played by two teams, each consisting of not more than five players, one of whom is the goalkeeper.

一场比赛应有两队参加，每队上场球员不得多于 5 人，其中一人必须为守门员。

A match may not start if either team consists of fewer than three players.

如果任何一队少于 3 人则比赛不能开始。

The match is abandoned if one of the teams has fewer than three players on the pitch.

在比赛中，任何一队在场上队员人数少于 3 人（包括守门员），比赛将被终止。

Up to a maximum of seven substitutes may be used in any match played in an official competition organised under the auspices of FIFA, the confederations or the member associations.

在由国际足联、洲际联合会或国家足协主办的任何正式比赛中，每场比赛最多可以使用 7 名替补队员。

The number of substitutions that may be made during a match is unlimited.

比赛中使用的替换次数不受限制。

In national "A" team matches, up to a maximum of ten substitutes may be used.

在国家 A 级比赛中，最多可使用 10 名替补队员。

In all other matches, a greater number of substitutes may be used, provided that:

- the teams concerned reach agreement on a maximum number
- the referees are informed before the match

在其他所有比赛中，只要符合下列条件即可使用更多数量的替补队员：

- 比赛双方就替补人数达成一致意见
- 比赛前通知裁判员

If the referees are not informed, or if no agreement is reached before the match, no more than ten substitutes are allowed.

如果赛前没有通知裁判员，或双方未达成一致意见，替补队员人数不得超过 10 人。

In all matches, the names of the players and substitutes must be given to the referees prior to the start of the match, whether they are present or not. Any substitute whose name is not given to the referees at this time may not take part in the match.

在所有比赛中，无论他们在场与否，首发队员和替补队员名单必须在比赛开始前交给裁判员。在赛前规定时间内，任何没有提交给裁判员名单的替补队员不得参加比赛。

9.5 A Glossary of Sport in English and Chinese

边线 touch line
裁判 referee
对手 opponent
罚出场 send off
罚球点 penalty spot
罚点球 penalty kick
罚球区域 penalty area
防守者 defender
非越位位置 onside position
更衣室 dressing room
观众 spectator
核对名单 checking of registration
横木 crossbar
基本装备 basic equipment
进球 goal scored
警告 caution
竞赛规程 competition rule
开球 kick-off
旗杆 flagposts
球场表面 field surface
球场界线 marking of the field
球门 goal
球门区域 goal area
球门网 goal net
球门线 goal line
球门柱 goal post
球鞋 footwear
球员号码 player's number
球在比赛外 ball out of play
球在比赛中 ball in play
驱离出场 explusion
哨子 whistle
胜队 winning team
守门员 goalkeeper
受伤球员 injured player

提出登记名单 presentation of registration
替补队员 substitute
越位位置 offside position
运动场 stadium
中点 centre spot
中圈 centre circle
中线旗 half-way flag
重新比赛 restart of play
助理裁判 assistant referee
坠球 drop ball
总教练 head coach

Chapter 10 Contrast of Sino-Western Cultures and Chinese-English Translation Texts in the Field of Science and Technology

10.1 What Are Science and Technology

Science and technology, often closely related, are two distinct subjects.

Science is a systematic enterprise that builds and organizes knowledge in the form of testable explanations and predictions about nature and the universe.

Technology is the collection of techniques, methods or processes used in the production of goods or services or in the accomplishment of objectives, such as scientific investigation.

Here is a chart of comparison:

	Science	**Technology**
Motto	Science is knowing	Technology is doing
Mission	The search for and theorizing about cause	The search for and theorizing about new processes
Result relevance	Making virtually value-free statements	Activities are always value-laden
Evaluation methods	Analysis, generalization and creation of theories	Analysis and synthesis of design
Goals achieved through	Corresponding scientific processes	Key technological processes
Focus	Focuses on understanding natural phenomena	Focuses on understanding the made environment
Development Methods	Discovery (controlled by experimentation)	Design, invention, production
Most observed quality	Drawing correct conclusions based on good theories and accurate data	Taking good decisions based on incomplete data and approximate models
Skills needed to excel	Experimental and logical skills	Design, construction, testing, planning, quality assurance, problem solving, decision making, interpersonal and communication skills

10.2 Cultural Contrast of Science and Technology in China and the West

10.2.1 Science and Technology in China

China was a world leader in science and technology until the early years of the Qing Dynasty. Chinese discoveries and Chinese innovations such as paper making, printing, compass, and gunpowder (the Four Great Inventions) contributed to the economic development in Asia and Europe. Chinese activity started to decrease in the fourteenth century.

Unlike in Europe, Chinese scientists did not attempt to reduce observations of nature to mathematical laws and did not form a scholarly community with criticisms and progressive research. There was an increasing concentration on literature, arts, and public administration while science and technology were seen as trivial or restricted to limited practical applications. The causes of this Great Divergence continue to be debated. One factor is argued to be the imperial examination system which removed the incentives for Chinese intellectuals to learn mathematics or to conduct experimentation.

After being defeated repeatedly by Western nations in the 19th century, Chinese reformers began promoting modern science and technology as part of the Self-Strengthening Movement.

After 1949 science and technology research was organized based on the model of the Soviet Union. Science and technology was established as one of the Four Modernizations in 1976. Deng Xiaoping, the architect of the Chinese economic reform, was a strong promoter of science and technology, as a result China scored substantial progress in many fields.

10.2.2 Science and Technology in the West

Science and technology in the United Kingdom has a long history, producing many important figures and developments in the field.

Major theorists from the UK include Isaac Newton whose laws of motion and illumination of gravity have been seen as a keystone of modern science and Charles Darwin whose theory of evolution by natural selection was fundamental to the development of modern biology.

Major scientific discoveries include hydrogen by Henry Cavendish, penicillin by Alexander Fleming, and the structure of DNA by Francis Crick and others.

Major engineering projects and applications pursued by people from the UK include the steam locomotive developed by Richard Trevithick and Andrew Vivian, the jet engine by Frank Whittle and the World Wide Web by Tim Berners-Lee.

Scientific research and development remains important in British universities, with many establishing science parks to facilitate production and co-operation with industry. The UK plays a leading part in the aerospace industry, with companies including Rolls-Royce playing a leading role in the aero-engine market; BAE Systems acting as Britain's largest and the Pentagon's sixth largest defence supplier, and large companies including GKN acting as major suppliers to the Airbus project. Two British-based companies, Glaxo Smith Kline and Astra Zeneca, ranked in the top five pharmaceutical companies in the world by sales in 2009 and UK companies have discovered and developed more leading medicines than any other country apart from the US.

The United States Constitution itself reflects the desire to encourage scientific creativity. It gives the United States Congress the power "to promote the progress of science and useful arts, by securing for limited times to authors and inventors the exclusive right to their respective writings and discoveries." This clause formed the basis for the U.S. patent and copyright systems, whereby creators of original art and technology would get a government granted monopoly, which after a limited period would become free to all citizens, thereby enriching the public domain.

During the 19th century, Britain, France, and Germany were at the forefront of new ideas in science and mathematics. The United States excelled in using theory to solve problems: applied science. This tradition had been born of necessity. Because Americans lived so far from the well-springs of Western science and manufacturing, they often had to figure out their own ways of doing things. When Americans combined theoretical knowledge with "Yankee ingenuity," the result was a flow of important inventions. The great American inventors include Robert Fulton (the steamboat); Samuel Morse (the telegraph); Eli Whitney (the cotton gin); Cyrus McCormick (the reaper); and Thomas Alva Edison, the most fertile of them all, with more than a thousand inventions credited to his name.

Edison was not always the first to devise a scientific application, but he was frequently the one to bring an idea to a practical finish. For example, the British engineer Joseph Swan built an incandescent electric lamp in 1860, almost 20 years before Edison. But Edison's light bulbs lasted much longer than Swan's, and they could be turned on and off individually, while Swan's bulbs could be used only in a system where several lights were turned on or off at the same time. Edison followed up his improvement of the light bulb with the development of electrical generating systems. Within 30 years, his inventions had introduced electric lighting into millions of homes.

Another landmark application of scientific ideas to practical uses was the innovation of the brothers Wilbur and Orville Wright. In the 1890s they became fascinated with accounts of German glider experiments and began their own investigation into the principles of flight. Combining scientific knowledge and mechanical skills, the Wright brothers built and flew several gliders. Then, on December 17, 1903, they successfully flew the first heavier-than-air, mechanically propelled airplane.

An American invention that was barely noticed in 1947 went on to usher in the Information Age. In that year John Bardeen, William Shockley, and Walter Brattain of Bell Laboratories drew upon highly sophisticated principles of quantum physics to invent the transistor, a small substitute for the bulky vacuum tube. This, and a device invented 10 years later, the integrated circuit, made it possible to package enormous amounts of electronics into tiny containers. As a result, book-sized computers of today can outperform room-sized computers of the 1960s, and there has been a revolution in the way people live — in how they work, study, conduct business, and engage in research.

10.3 Chinese-English Translation Texts in the Field of Science and Technology

10.3.1 Nouns or Pronouns, Short Sentences or Lengthy Ones

Chinese and English have different tendencies for expressing nominal entities: In Chinese more full nouns are used while in English more pronouns are used, including personal pronouns such as *we*, *you*, *he* and *they* and relational pronouns in introducing attributive clauses such as *that*, *which*, *who*, *whom*, *whose*.

The tendency for nouns or pronouns systematically produces another tendency in sentence structure: Chinese prefers short sentences while English uses lengthy ones more often.

Lengthy sentences have two or more than two clauses with one subordinating to another or one coordinating with another. This produces the opportunities for using pronouns in a later clause whose antecedent appears in the preceding clause.

Short sentences, as a contrast, stand on their own with fewer connections with surrounding clauses, and the context for the use of pronoun fails as a consequence. So, the preference for full nouns and that for short sentences are symbiotic (共生) phenomena, while the preference for pronouns and that for lengthy sentences coexist.

(1) Zoology is still a minority subject in universities, and even those who choose to study it often make their decision without appreciating its profound philosophical significance.

在大学里，动物学仍是少数人研究的课题，即使那些决定选学这门课的人，往往也不是出于赏识其深刻的哲学意义。

In (1), four pronouns or their possessive forms are used; they serve as a kind of glue to link together the otherwise separate chunks of words, hence a lengthy sentence. The Chinese version uses 这门课 and 人 to replace the pronouns *it* and *those who* respectively.

And as a result, the lengthy sentence is broken apart.

(2) Therefore we must expect that when we go and look at the behaviour of baboons, humans, and all other living creatures, we shall find it to be selfish.

因此我们可以预见到，当我们去观察狒狒、人类和其他一切生物的行为时，一定会发现它们的行为是自私的。

In (2), the pronoun *that* introduces a complement clause, producing a complex and lengthy sentence. In the Chinese version it is vacant, therefore the complex and lengthy sentence gives way to short ones. Also, *it* is transformed into 行为, a nominalized word.

More examples can be found in (3) and (4) where pronouns *that*, *who* and *what* are used making the clauses which they belong with or which they lead much more lengthy than their Chinese counterparts.

(3) My own feeling is that a human society based simply on the gene's law of universal ruthless selfishness would be a very nasty society in which to live.

我自己也觉得，一个单纯以基因那种普遍的、无情的自私性法则为基础的人类社会，生活在其中将会令人厌恶之极。

(4) I stress this, because I know I am in danger of being misunderstood by those people, all too numerous, who cannot distinguish a statement of belief in what is the case from an advocacy of what ought to be the case.

我之所以强调这一点，因为我知道我有被人误解的危险。有些人不能把阐述对事物的认识同提倡事物应该如何这两件事区别开来，此类人为数实在太多。

10.3.2 Front Weight or End Weight

Front weight means that, in Chinese, more words appear as modifiers before the head, while end weight means the reverse structure: lengthy modifiers come behind the head. Let's see (5) and (6).

(5) To be fair, others had had inklings of the truth, but it was Darwin who first put together a coherent and tenable account of why we exist.

说句公道话，其他的人对事实真相也曾有过一些模糊的想法，但对于我们之所以存在的道理第一个做了有条理、站得住脚的阐述的却是达尔文。

(6) Living organisms had existed on earth, without ever knowing why, for over three thousand million years before the truth finally dawned on one of them.

三十多亿年来，地球上一直存在着各种活的有机体，但对生命存在的道理，它们始终一无所知。

In (5), the underlined lengthy modifier comes behind the head *Darwin*. This is what we call end weight. But in Chinese 达尔文 is the head whose modifier comes before it, where front weight exists.

In (6), the phrase *without ever knowing* has a very lengthy complement behind it while in Chinese all words before 一无所知 is the content, which is a front weight structure.

10.4 Samples

4K standards will probably double current image frame rates, to a 120 fps maximum. Higher frame rates mean greater image clarity and smoother motion, but these benefits haven't always been able to sell themselves.

4K 标准有可能让如今的照片帧率翻倍,最大达到 120fps。帧率更高意味着图片清晰度更高、动作更流畅,但这些优点可能无法成为卖点。

When *The Hobbit*: *An Unexpected Journey* was released in 48 frames-per-second (double the 24fps that film buffs have experienced for their entire lives) in selected theaters (with compatible projects), it was meant to enhance 3D image clarity, which by all accounts it did, but in a way that many found subjectively unpleasant, so much so in fact that the higher-frame rate was cancelled for the two sequels.

《霍比特人 1: 意外之旅》在一些有兼容放映机的影院里按 48fps 的帧率播放,而电影爱好者们毕生只体验过 24fps 的清晰度。高帧率意味着 3D 画面的清晰度提高了,但事实上,这却并未广受好评。因此接下来两部都没有采用高帧率。

The complaints? That the image seemed fake, unnatural, hyper-real, surreal, or otherwise wrong. Is this valid? Of course not. Higher-frame rates are actually truer to life than lesser rates. Was the audience right to think it looked strange? Absolutely. 24 fps film is what we've all grown up with, so anything different is going to seem strange at first. Higher frame rates provide smooth motion in a way that seems "a little too perfect" to the uninitiated. Can we adapt? Possibly.

为何没有受到好评呢?人们反映图片看着太假、不自然、过于真实反而显得不真实。这样的说法有根据吗?当然没有。高帧率比低帧率更接近实际生活。那观众认为高帧率看起来奇怪说得通吗?当然也说得通。因为我们从小看着 24fps 的电影长大,与之不同的电影起初会让人们感到奇怪。高帧率带来的流畅的动作一定程度上让人们感到有点过于完美。那么人们能接受 48fps 吗?也许吧。

Music lovers who grew up with vinyl records often complain that CD's sound a little chilly, sterile, computerized, and otherwise overly precise, but that hasn't hindered the rise of digital formats in any serious way.

对于音乐爱好者来说,听黑胶唱片长大的人觉得 CD 的音质有点冰冷、乏味、机械化,又过于精确,但这并未阻挡数字音乐兴起的步伐。

Hollywood isn't giving up either, with *Billy Lynne's Long Halftime Walk* from acclaimed filmmaker Ang Lee slated to be the first 120fps feature film in history, and James Cameron's *Avatar* sequels also rumoured for higher frame-rate immersion.

好莱坞也没有放弃高帧率,大导演李安拍摄的《比利·林恩的中场战事》被誉为史上第一部 120fps 的故事片,詹姆斯·卡梅隆执导的《阿凡达》续集据说也会采用高帧率。

10.5 A Glossary of Science and Technology in English and Chinese

产生深远的影响 exert a far-reaching impact on...
创新的 innovative
促进相关产业发展 promote relative industries
打下良好的基础 lay a solid foundation for...
恶化 aggravate
翻天覆地的改变 earth-shaking changes
废气 exhaust gas
负面影响 negative forces
过度商业化 over-commercialized
航空旅行 air travel
环保的能源 environmentally-friendly resources
尖端的 cutting-edge
尖端科学 advanced science
尖端设备 sophisticated equipment
交通工具 transportation tools
科技创新 technical innovation
科技进步 technological progress/advances
科学发明 scientific invention
科学探索 scientific exploration
可持续性发展 sustainable development
可替代燃料 alternative fuel
克服困难 overcome difficulties
里程碑 milestone
能源危机 energy crisis
能源消耗 depletion of resources
前所未有的 unprecedented
潜在危险 potential hazards
取得进步 make progress
取得突破性进展 see dramatic breakthroughs

上瘾 be addicted to/be obsessed with
社会地位 social status
双刃剑 double-edged sword
提高生产效率 augment/enhance/boost/ efficiency/productivity
性价比高的 cost-effective

Chapter 11 Contrast of Sino-Western Cultures and Chinese-English Translation Texts in the Field of Medicine

11.1 What Is Medicine

Medicine is the science and practice of the diagnosis, treatment, and prevention of disease. The word *medicine* is derived from Latin *medicus*, meaning "a physician." Medicine encompasses a variety of health care practices evolved to maintain and restore health by the prevention and treatment of disease.

Prescientific forms of medicine are now known as traditional medicine and folk medicine. They remain commonly used with or instead of scientific medicine and are thus called alternative medicine.

Contemporary medicine applies biomedical sciences, biomedical research, genetics, and medical technology to diagnose, treat, and prevent injury and disease, typically through pharmaceuticals or surgery, but also through therapies as diverse as psychotherapy, external splints and traction, medical devices, biologics, and ionizing radiation, amongst others.

11.2 Cultural Contrast of Medicine in China and the West

11.2.1 Medicine in China

Traditional Chinese Medicine (TCM) is a broad range of medicine practices sharing common concepts which have been developed in China and are based on a tradition of more than 2,000 years, including various forms of herbal medicine, acupuncture, massage, exercise, and dietary therapy. It is primarily used as a complementary alternative medicine approach. TCM is widely used in China and it is also used in the West.

TCM holds that the body's vital energy (qi) circulates through channels, called meridians, that have branches connected to bodily organs and functions. Concepts of the body and of disease used in TCM reflect its origins in pre-scientific culture, similar to European humoral theory. Scientific investigation has found no histological or physiological evidence for traditional Chinese concepts such as qi, meridians, and acupuncture points.

TCM's view of the body places little emphasis on anatomical structures, but is mainly concerned with the identification of functional entities (which regulate digestion, breathing, aging etc). While health is perceived as harmonious interaction of these entities and the outside world, disease is interpreted as a disharmony in interaction. TCM diagnosis aims to trace symptoms to patterns of an underlying disharmony, by measuring the pulse, inspecting the tongue, skin, and eyes, and looking at the eating and sleeping habits of the person as well as many other things.

Traces of therapeutic activities in China date from the Shang dynasty (14th—11th centuries BC). Though the Shang did not have a concept of "medicine" as distinct from other fields, their oracular inscriptions on bones and tortoise shells refer to illnesses that affected the Shang royal family: eye disorders, toothaches, bloated abdomen, etc. which Shang elites usually attributed to curses sent by their ancestors. There is no evidence that the Shang nobility used herbal remedies. According to a 2006 overview, the documentation of Chinese materia medica (CMM) dates back to around 1100 BC when only dozens of drugs were first described. By the end of the 16th century, the number of drugs documented had reached close to 1,900. And by the end of the last century, published records of CMM have reached 12,800 drugs.

Stone and bone needles found in ancient tombs led Joseph Needham to speculate that acupuncture might have been carried out in the Shang dynasty. But most historians now make a distinction between medical lancing (or bloodletting) and acupuncture in the narrower sense of using metal needles to treat illnesses by stimulating specific points along circulation channels (i. e. meridians) in accordance with theories related to the circulation of qi. The earliest public evidence for acupuncture in this sense dates to the second or first century BC.

The doctrines of Chinese medicine are rooted in books such as the *Yellow Emperor's Inner Canon* and the *Treatise on Cold Damage*, as well as in cosmological notions such as yin-yang and the five phases. *The Compendium of Materia Medica* (《本草纲目》) published in 1603 is a pharmaceutical text written by Li Shizhen (1518—1593 AD) during the Ming dynasty of China.

11.2.2 Medicine in the West

The practice of medicine changed with the rapid advances of science, as well as new approaches by physicians. Hospital doctors began much more systematic analysis of patients' symptoms in diagnosis. Among the more powerful new techniques were anaesthesia, and the development of both antiseptic and aseptic operating theatres. Actual cures were developed for certain endemic infectious diseases. However, the decline in many of the most lethal diseases was more due to improvements in public health and nutrition than to medicine.

Medicine was revolutionized in the 19th century and beyond by advances in chemistry and laboratory techniques and equipment, old ideas of infectious disease epidemiology were replaced with bacteriology and virology.

During the First World War, Alexis Carrel and Henry Dakin developed the Carrel-Dakin method of treating wounds with an irrigation, Dakin's solution, a germicide which helped prevent gangrene. It also spurred the usage of Roentgen's X-ray, and the electrocardiograph, for the monitoring of internal bodily functions. This was followed in the inter-war period by the development of the first anti-bacterial agents such as the sulpha antibiotics.

The World Health Organization (WHO) was founded in 1948 as a United Nations agency to improve global health. In most of the world, life expectancy has improved since then, and was about 67 years as of 2010, and well above 80 years in some countries. Eradication of infectious diseases is an international effort, and several new vaccines have been developed during the post-war years, against infections such as measles, mumps, several strains of influenza and human papilloma virus. The long-known vaccine against smallpox finally eradicated the disease in the 1970s, and rinderpest was wiped out in 2011. X-ray imaging was the first kind of medical imaging, and later ultrasonic imaging, CT scanning, MR scanning and other imaging methods became available.

Genetics have advanced with the discovery of the DNA molecule, genetic mapping and gene therapy. Stem cell research took off after the year 2000.

11.3 Chinese-English Translation Texts in the Field of Medicine

11.3.1 Discriminating Technical Terms from Daily Uses

As we have observed above, the Chinese language has a lesser degree of abstraction, so everyday language is used in the field of medicine without making any discrimination. But when they are translated into English which embraces a good tradition of making abstractions in thinking, technical words have to be chosen to discriminate them from daily talk.

(1) 望闻问切

inspection, auscultation(听诊) and olfaction(嗅觉), inquiring, and palpation(触诊)

In (1), 望闻问切 are what we actually perform in daily life, but in English *looking*, *hearing-smelling*, *asking* and *touching* are not good choices. More technical words are *inspection*, *auscultation and olfaction*, *inquiring*, and *palpation*.

(2) 中风是以突然昏仆、不省人事,或半身不遂、语言不利、口角歪斜为主的一种疾病。因其起病急骤、变化多端,与风性善行数变的特征相似,故类比称为"中风"。

Wind stroke is an emergency case manifested by falling down in a fit with loss of consciousness, or hemiplegia(偏瘫), slurred speech and deviated mouth. It is characterized by abrupt onset with pathological changes varying quickly like the wind, from which the term "wind stroke" comes.

Also in (2), the daily words in Chinese are rendered into medicine terms to cope with some particular field of language use.

11.3.2 Explicit or Implicit Use of Modality

In English, modal words such as *should*, *must*, *can*, *would* are frequenly used to show the speaker's judgment of usuality, frequency, possibility and degree of obligation. The Chinese culture is known for its being implicit in speaking. Keeping your true sentiment unknown has been a warning from generation to generation. As a reflection in language, modal words are less often used to conceal the speaker's true feelings or true judgments and the addressee is left free to figure out the modality of the speaker, sometimes a correct estimation, sometimes a faulty one. The examples below have modal verbs in English but none in Chinese.

(3) 重阴必阳,重阳必阴。

Extreme yin will necessarily produce yang and vice versa.

(4) 阴无阳不生,阳无阴不长。

Without yang there would be no production of yin. Without yin there would be no production of yang.

12.3.3 English Featuring Hypotaxis, Chinese Parataxis

English uses a lot of conjunctions to link up the clauses, thus making English sentences structurally comlex with robust coherence. The Chinese language relies on semantic coherece to build up connections between adjoining clauses, and there are few linguistic devices used as cohesive devices.

In (5), the conjunction *if* is used to show the hypothetical condition in the English version but in Chinese it is a default value.

(5) 医者在针刺过程中,发现患者面色苍白,出汗或诉说头晕时,这是晕针的表现,应及时采取处理措施。

During the treatment, if there appear some symptoms of fainting, such as pallor, sweating or dizziness, management should be taken promptly.

Similarly in the examples below, juxtaposed constructions are used without cohesive devices of any sort to link up the short clauses, which is typical parataxis. But in English, complex structures are used to translate the short clauses. Non-predicate phrases (gerund, infinitive or participle) or attributive clauses work as subsidiary structures to achieve hypotaxis.

(6) 取胃之募穴和足阳明经穴为主，针用泻法，以消食化滞，和胃止痛。

The Front-Mu point of the stomach and the point of Stomach Meridian are treated with reducing manipulation to remove food retention to pacify the stomach and (to) relieve pain.

(7) 肾主骨生髓充脑，其华在发。

The kidney dominates bone, manufactures marrow(髓) to fill up the brain and manifests in the hair.

(8) 过饥、过饱、醉酒、劳累过度时，不宜立即进行针刺。

It is advisable not to give acupuncture treatment to those who are either hungry, overeaten, drunk or overfatigued.

11.3.4 English Favoring the Passive Voice, Chinese the Active

In English passive voice is more often used than in Chinese. In Chinese the active voice may express the meaning of being passive, which remind us of parataxis(意合). English resorts to full-fledged grammatical means, exemplifying how hypotaxis(形合) is used. Let's see the examples below:

(9) 取任脉经穴为主，重用灸法，以回阳固脱。

Moxibustion is applied to the points of Conception Vessel to restore yang from collapse.

(10) 针刺操作，需双手协作进行。右手持针，进行针刺操作，称为刺手；左手按压穴位局部，帮助针刺，称为押手。

The needle should be inserted coordinately with the help of both hands. Generally it is held with the right hand known as the puncturing hand. The left hand known as the pressing hand pushes firmly against the area close to the point.

(11) 虚则补之，实则泻之。

Reinforcing is applied in case of deficiency. The excess syndrome is treated by the reducing method.

11.3.5 Techniques in Translating from Chinese into English

In translating Chinese discourses of traditional Chinese medicine into Enlish, a large package of techniques are used, including literal, liberal, a combination of both, loan, paraphrase, among others.

Examples of literal translation:

(12) 木生火，火生土。

Wood promotes fire. Fire promotes earth.

(13) 精血互生。

Essence and blood are mutually generated.

(14) 肝藏血。

The liver stores blood.

(15) 脾为生痰之源。

The spleen is the source of phlegm production.

Examples of liberal translation:

(16) 通脉活络。

Remove obstruction from the meridians and collaterals.

(17) 开窍醒脑。

Promote resuscitation(复苏).

In (16), the two parallel structures of 通脉 and 活络 are translated into one VO structure. The contrast in (17) is identical.

Examples of transliteration:

(18) 阴阳、经络、气、三焦、百会、脏腑

Yinyang, Jingluo, Qi, Sanjiao, Baihui, Zangfu

Examples of transliteration and liberal translation:

(19) 原气、络穴、手阳明大肠经

Yuan primary qi, Luo-connecting point, the Large Intestine Meridian of Hand Yangming

In (19), 气 and 阳明 are transliterated, while others are liberally translated.

Examples of loan translation from western medical terminologies:

(20) 瘦病、耳针疗法

goiter(甲状腺肿), auricular(耳的) therapy

Examples of paraphrasing:

(21) 五脏

five storing viscera (heart, liver, spleen, lung and kidney)

(22) 六腑

six excreting viscera (gallbladder, stomach, small intestine, large intestine, sanjiao and bladder)

(23) 七情

seven emotions (joy, anger, worry, anxiety, sadness, fear and fright)

11.4 Sample

《黄帝内经》(节选)

Yellow Emperor's Classics of Internal Medicine (Excerpt)

四气调神大论篇第二

Chapter 2: Great Treatise on Regulation of Spirit in Harmony with the Climates of Four Seasons

春三月，此谓发陈。天地俱生，万物以荣，夜卧早起，广步于庭，被发缓形，以使志生，生而勿杀，予而勿夺，赏而勿罚，此春气之应，养生之道也；逆之则伤肝，夏为实寒变，奉长者少。

The three months of spring are the period in which things begin to grow and display. Heaven begins to generate warm energy and Earth begins to develop, so that everything flourishes. It is desirable to sleep at night, get up early in the morning, take a walk in the yard, to loosen up hair and relax the body. The spring possesses the will to grow, and after things have grown, do not destroy them. In spring, one should assist instead of taking it away; one should praise instead of punishing. This is the way of nourishing life in response to the spring. To act to the contrary will cause injuries to the liver and one will suffer a cold disease in summer.

夏三月，此谓蕃秀。天地气交，万物华实，夜卧早起，无厌于日，使志勿怒，使华英成秀，使气得泄，若所爱在外，此夏气之应，养长之道也；逆之则伤心，秋为痎疟，奉收者少，冬至重病。

The three months of summer are the period in which things become flourishing and beautiful. The energy of Heaven and that of Earth begin to interact with each other so that everything begins to blossom and bear fruits. It is desirable to sleep at night and get up early in the morning, to have no dislike of sunlight, possess no will of anger, so that things will be blooming beautifully and so that energy will move outward through perspiration as if in love with the outside world. This is is the way of nourishing life in response to the summer. To act to the contrary will cause injuries to the heart and one will suffer malaria that attacks every other day in the autumn, because he is bound to be short of energy to cope with the autumn.

秋三月，此谓容平，天气以急，地气以明，早卧早起，与鸡俱兴，使志安宁，以缓秋刑，收敛神气，使秋气平，无外其志，使肺气清，此秋气之应，养收之道也；逆之则伤肺，冬为飧泄，奉藏者少。

The three months of autumn are the period in which the shapes of everything are formed. The energy of Heaven begins to blow swiftly, the energy of Earth begins to change color. It is desirable to sleep early and get up early with the crowing of the rooster, to maintain a peaceful will in order to slow down the killing effects of autumn, to constrict the energy of spirits in order to calm down the energy of autumn, to refrain from moving outward in order to clean up the energy of lungs. This is the way of nourishing life in response to the energy of autumn. To act to the contrary will cause injuries to the lungs and one will suffer diarrhea with undigested foods in winter, because one will be bound to be short of energy to cope with the winter.

冬三月，此谓闭藏。水冰地坼，勿扰乎阳，早卧晚起，必待日光，使志若伏若匿，若有私意，若已有得，去寒就温，无泄皮肤，使气极夺。此冬气之应，养藏之道也；逆之则伤肾，春为痿厥，奉生者少。

The three months of winter are the period in which everything is closed and stored. Water freezes and the earth cracks, so that Yang remains dormant not to be disturbed. It is desirable to sleep early and get up late, to await the arrival of sunlight, so that the will remains dormant as if hiding or pretending, not unlike someone with private intentions, not unlike someone with all his desires already fulfilled. In winter, one should avoid cold and remain warm and refrain from perspiring so that Yang energy will not be frequently attacked by cold energy. This is the way of nourishing life in response to the energy of winter. To act to the contrary will cause injuries to the kidneys and one will suffer weakened limbs in spring, because he is bound to be short of energy to cope with the spring.

天气清净，光明者也，藏德不止，故不下也。

The energy of Heaven is clear and bright. It contains indefinite sources of virtues and it will never descend so is true energy in man which contains indefinite sources of power and it is never used up.

天明则日月不明，邪害空窍。阳气者闭塞，地气者冒明，云雾不精，则上应白露不下。交通不表，万物命故不施，不施则名木多死。恶气不发，风雨不节，白露不下，则菀槁不荣。贼风数至，暴雨数起，天地四时不相保，与道相失，则未央绝灭。

When Heaven gives away its brightness it will outmatch the brightness of the sun and the moon, and man' s openings will suffer as a result, because the energy of Heaven (namely, wind and heat) will block up the nine openings of man and the energy of Earth (including dampness, clouds and fog) will block up man's vision; moreover, the purity of the clouds and fog will not come about with the result that they will fail to bring down white dew from Heaven. Under such circumstances, interaction between Heaven and Earth (between Yin and Yang) does not take shape, and everything will lose its source of life leading to the death of most famous fruits and precious trees. As the vicious energy fails to disperse, wind and rain become excessive and unchecked, white dew fails to descend, withering trees will pile up and the spring will not flourish. Stealing wind will blow frequently, heavy rain will fall constantly, and the four seasons will lose their protection. This is contrary to the Tao that has been lost, and everything will soon be destroyed.

唯圣人从之，故身无奇病，万物不失，生气不竭。逆春气则少阳不生，肝气内变。逆夏气则太阳不长，心气内洞。逆秋气则太阴不收，肺气焦满。逆冬气则少阴不藏，肾气独沉。

Only the sages are able to live in harmony with the Tao, so that they will not be under the attack of strange diseases, they do not lose anything in their possession, and their life energy is never exhausted. To live against the trends of spring energy will block up the birth of little Yang which moves inward to cause the disease of liver. To live against the trends of summer energy will obstruct the growth of great Yang which moves inward to deprive the heart of its energy. To live against the trends of autumn energy will lead to an inability of great Yin to constrict which brings about energy congestion of lungs in the upper burning space. To live against the trends of winter energy will lead to an inability of little Yin to store which brings about a descending of kidneys energy.

夫四时阴阳者，万物之根本也。所以圣人春夏养阳，秋冬养阴，以从其根；故与万物沉浮于生长之门，逆其根则伐其本，坏其真矣。故阴阳四时者，万物之终始也；生死之本也；逆之则灾害生，从之则苛疾不起，是谓得道。

The four seasons and Yin and Yang are the fundamentals of everything, and for that reason, the sages nourish Yang in spring and summer, and they nourish Yin in autumn and winter, in order to act upon the fundamentals (the roots). This is why the sages are capable of living in harmony with everything surrounding them. To live against the roots means to deprive oneself of the source of life and to destroy one's true energy. Therefore, Yin, Yang, and the four seasons are the beginnings and the ends of everything. They are the roots of life and death; to live against them will bring about destruction of life, and to live in harmony with them will prevent disease which is called accomplishing the way of nourishing life (accomplishment of Tao).

道者，圣人行之，愚者佩之。从阴阳则生，逆之则死；从之则治，逆之则乱。反顺为逆，是谓内格。是故圣人不治已病治未病，不治已乱治未乱，此之谓也。夫病已成而后药之，乱已成而后治之，譬犹渴而穿井，斗而铸锥，不亦晚乎？

A sage will act upon Tao, but a fool will only admire it. To live in harmony with Yin and Yang means life and to live against Yin and Yang means death; to live in harmony with Yin and Yang will bring about peace, and to live against Yin and Yang will bring about chaos. To live against Yin and Yang which should be obeyed results from the internal resistance to the way of Heaven. Therefore, the sages will prevent disease rather than cure it, maintain order rather than correcting disorder, which is the ultimate principle of wisdom. To cure a disease with medicines or to correct a disorder is like digging a well when one already feels thirsty or making weapons when the war has already broken out, which is too late to do much good.

11.5 A Glossary of Medicine in English and Chinese

安神法 tranquillization method
标本兼治 treating both manifestation and root cause of disease
表里分消 eliminating pathogens by diaphoresis and purgation respectively
表里双解 expelling pathogens from both interior and exterior
补脾益肺 invigorating spleen for benefiting lung
补血养心 replenishing blood for nourishing heart
补阳 tonifying yang
补益法 invigoration method
补益脾肾 invigorating spleen and kidney
除湿通络 eliminating dampness and dredging channels
疮疡补法 benefiting method for sore and ulcer
涤痰息风 clearing phlegm for calming endogenous wind
调和肝脾 harmonizing liver and spleen
反治法 retrograde treatment
芳香化湿 resolving of dampness with aromatics
芳香化浊 eliminating turbid pathogen with aromatics
分消走泄 diaphoresis, purgation and diuresis
扶正固本 strengthening body resistance
甘温除热 relieving high fever with sweet and warm-natured drugs
攻补兼施 reinforcement and elimination in combination
攻下冷积 treating coagulated cold by purgation
攻下逐瘀 eliminating blood stasis by catharsis
固表止汗 consolidating exterior for arresting sweating
寒因寒用 treating false-cold syndrome with cold-natured drugs
和解表里 reconciling exterior and interior
和胃降逆 regulating stomach for lowering adverse qi
化湿和中 removing dampness for regulating stomach
缓则治本 radical treatment in chronic case
回阳生肌 restoring yang and promoting granulation

活血调经 promoting blood flow for regulating menstruation
急则治标 symptomatic treatment in acute condition
健脾化湿 invigorating spleen for eliminating dampness
解表法 resolving exterior method
解毒护阴 removing toxin for protecting yin
开窍法 inducing resuscitation method
苦温燥湿 dispelling dampness with bitter and warm-natured drugs
理气法 regulating qi-flowing method
理气和胃 regulating qi-flowing for harmonizing stomach
利水消肿 inducing diuresis for removing edema
敛疮止痛 healing sore and rlieving pain
凉血化瘢 cooling blood for resolving macula
明目 improving eyesight
内治法 internal treatment
宁心开窍 calming heart for resuscitation
暖肝散寒 warming liver for dispelling cold
暖宫散寒 warming uterus for dispelling cold; warming womb for dispelling cold
平调寒热 mildly regulating cold and heat
平肝降逆 suppressing hyperactive liver for lowering adverse qi
破瘀散结 removing blood stasis and resolving static blood
清肺润燥 clearing lung-heat and moistening dryness
清肝明目 removing liver fire for improving eyesight
驱虫法 expelling intestinal parasites method
祛风化痰 dispelling pathogenic wind and eliminating phlegm
去毒生肌 detoxication and promoting granulation
热者寒之 treating heat syndrome with cold natured drugs
柔肝息风 softening liver for calming endogenous wind
润肺止咳 moistening lung for arresting cough
润燥法 moistening dryness method
塞因塞用 treating obstructive syndrome with tonifying method
散寒除湿 dispelling cold and removing dampness
涩肠止泻 relieving diarrhea with astringents
杀虫消疳 destroying parasites for curing malnutrition
渗湿利水 eliminating dampness to promote diuresis
生肌定痛 promoting granulation and relieving pain
实者泻之 treating excess syndrome with purgative method
疏风透疹 dispelling wind to promote eruption
疏肝和胃 dispersing stagnated liver qi for regulating stomach

舒筋活络 relieving rigidity of muscles and activating collaterals
提脓拔毒 elminating pus and toxin
通耳 improving hearing
通腑排脓 catharsis and expelling pus
同病异治 treating same disease with different methods
温补脾阳 warmly invigorating spleen yang
温补肾阳 warming and recuperating kidney yang
息风定痫 arresting epilepsy by calming endogenous wind
消食化滞 resolving food stagnation
泻下逐水 removing water retention by purgation
辛凉解表 resolving exterior with pungent and cool natured drugs
行气降逆 activating qi for lowering adverse qi
宣肺通气 dispersing lung qi
养血安神 nourishing blood for tranquillization
异病同治 treating different diseases with same method
益火消阴 boosting source of fire for eliminating abundance of yin
引火归原 conducting fire back to its origin
燥湿化痰 eliminating dampness and phlegm
治病求本 treatment aiming at its pathogenesis
滋补肺肾 nourishing lung and kidney
滋阴益胃 nourishing yin for benefiting stomach

Chapter 12 Contrast of Sino-Western Cultures and Chinese-English Translation Texts in the Field of Weather and Climate

12.1 What Are Weather and Climate

Weather is the state of the atmosphere, to the degree that it is hot or cold, wet or dry, calm or stormy, clear or cloudy. Most weather phenomena occur in the troposphere (对流层), just below the stratosphere(同温层). Weather refers to day-to-day temperature and precipitation activity, whereas climate is the term for the statistics of atmospheric conditions over longer periods of time. When used without qualification, *weather* is generally understood to mean the weather of the Earth.

Climate is the statistics of weather, usually over a 30-year interval. It is measured by assessing the patterns of variation in temperature, humidity, atmospheric pressure, wind, precipitation, atmospheric particle count and other meteorological variables in a given region over long periods of time. Climate differs from weather, in that weather only describes the short-term conditions of these variables in a given region.

12.2 Cultural Contrast of Weather and Climate in China and the West

12.2.1 Weather and Climate in China

China is a country with wide-ranging climatic conditions, so a description of China's weather and climate should be based on the region you plan to tour and the kind of weather you enjoy.

Autumn is normally the most comfortable season of the year. Spring roughly has the same average temperatures as autumn. Summer can be extremely hot and also a rainy season in China. Winter can be incredibly cold especially in the north.

In southeastern China, typoon is often a climatic disaster which brings too much rainfall and exerts a lot of damages to the areas it sweeps along. A typhoon is a mature tropical cyclone (旋风) that develops in the western part of the North Pacific Ocean. This region is referred to as the Northwestern Pacific Basin, and is the most active tropical cyclone basin, accounting for almost one-third of the world's annual tropical cyclones.

Beijing has a temperate and continental monsoon climate, with four distinct seasons and big differences in temperature between day and night. Summer in Beijing is hot and humid, while winter is cold and dry. Spring and autumn are short and cool. 75% of the annual precipitation is concentrated in summer from June to August, with frequent showers in July and August. The coldest month is January at an average of −4°C (25°F), and the hottest month is July at an average of 26°C (79°F).

The climate of Nanjing is more mild. The average annual temperature is about 15° C (60° F) and the time from mid-June to July is the rain period. Known as one of the four hottest cities in China, Nanjing's scorching summer period is to be avoided. The average ground temperature can reach 35° C (95°F) and the extreme highest point could reach 40°C (104°F) sometimes. The city's location at the lower river valley of the Yangtze River makes things worse as nearby mountains hold the hot air in. The short and comfortable autumn time from October to mid-November is the best travel period for the city. Unlike other southern cities in China, in December, it sometimes snows in the city. If fortunate, you will have an opportunity to appreciate the enthralling (迷人的) white snow world of Nanjing. In the coldest month — January, the temperature could be as low as −7°C (19°F).

12.2.2 Weather and Climate in the West

The climate in the United Kingdom is defined as a temperate oceanic climate, a classification it shares with most of north-west Europe. Regional climates are influenced by the Atlantic Ocean and latitude. Northern Ireland, Wales and western parts of England and Scotland, being closest to the Atlantic Ocean, are generally the mildest, wettest and windiest regions of the UK, and temperature ranges here are seldom extreme. Eastern areas are drier, cooler, less windy and also experience the greatest daily and seasonal temperature variations. Northern areas are generally cooler, wetter and have slightly larger temperature ranges than southern areas.

Though the UK is mostly under the influence of the maritime tropical air mass from the south-west, different regions are more susceptible than others when different air masses affect the country: Northern Ireland and the west of Scotland are the most exposed to the maritime polar air mass which brings cool moist air; the east of Scotland and north-east England are more exposed to the continental polar air mass which brings cold dry air; the south and south-east of England are more exposed to the continental tropical air mass which brings warm dry air (and consequently most of the time the warmest summer temperatures); and Wales and south-west England are the most exposed to the maritime tropical air mass which brings warm moist air.

The climate of the United States varies due to differences in latitude, and a range of geographic features, including mountains and deserts. West of the 100th meridian(西经

100 度以西地区), much of the US is semi-arid to arid, even desert in the far southwestern US. East of the 100th meridian, the climate is humid continental in the northern areas (locations above 40 north latitude, 北纬 40 度以北地区), to humid temperate in the central and middle Atlantic coast regions, to humid subtropical in the Gulf and south Atlantic regions. The southern tip of Florida is tropical. Higher-elevation areas of the Rocky Mountains, the Wasatch and Bighorn mountain ranges, the Sierra Nevada, and the Cascade Range are alpine. The climate along the coast of California is Merranean, while upper West Coast areas in coastal Oregon and Washington are cool temperate oceanic. The state of Alaska, on the northwestern corner of the North American continent, is largely subarctic, but with a cool oceanic climate in the southeast (Alaska Panhandle), southwestern peninsula and Aleutian Islands, and a polar climate in the north. The archipelago state of Hawaii, in the middle of the Pacific Ocean, is tropical, with rainfall concentrated in the cooler season (November to March). Tropical climates also prevail in US territories, which encompass Puerto Rico and various island archipelagoes, in the Samoan, Marianas and the US Virgin Islands.

As in most land masses located in the middle and lower-middle latitudes, the primary drivers of weather in the contiguous United States are the seasonal change in the solar angle, the migration north/south of the subtropical highs, and the seasonal change in the position of the polar jet stream. In the Northern Hemisphere summer, the "Bermuda High"(百慕大高压)over the subtropical Atlantic Ocean typically sends warm, humid air over the eastern, southern and central United States — resulting in southerly airflow, warm to hot temperatures, high humidity and occasional thunderstorm activity. In summer, high pressure over the north-central Pacific typically results in northwesterly airflow, stable conditions and cool to mild conditions along most of the immediate Pacific coast, from Washington state to San Diego, CA. In the Northern Hemisphere winter, the subtropical highs retreat southward. The polar jet stream (and associated conflict zone between cold, dry air masses from Canada and warm, moist air masses from the Gulf of Mexico) drops further southward into the United States — bringing major rain, ice and snow events, and much more variable, and sometimes dramatically colder, temperatures. Areas in the extreme southern US (Florida, the Gulf Coast, the Desert Southwest, and southern California) however, often have more stable weather, as the polar jet stream's impact does not usually reach that far south.

12.3 Chinese-English Translation Texts in the Field of Weather and Climate

12.3.1 Heavy Use of Technical Terms and Abbreviations

In meterological discourses, there is a heavy use of technical terms:

aerological theodolite：高空经纬仪
pyrheliometer：直接辐射表
pyranometer：总辐射表
anemorumbometer：风向风速表
aerosol particle size distribution：气溶胶粒子谱
monochromatic radiation：单色辐射
...

Abbreviations also abound as in other fields of science and technology discourses：

CB — cloud base：云底
DCP — data collection platform：资料收集平台
WEFAX — weather facsimile：天气图传真
CTH — cloud top height：云顶高度
Ci — cirrus：卷云
...

12.3.2 Ways of Voice Rendering

Ways of voice rendering between Chinese and English consists of three types.

English passive sentences are usually rendered into Chinese without a shift in voice. But Chinese passive voice takes advantage of a multiple lexical markers, apart from the most frequently used 被, many other markers such as 受，由，为，给，叫，靠，让，为……所 also take up a certain proportion.

(1) The laws of motion of the atmosphere may be expressed as a set of partial differential equations relating the instantaneous rate of change of the meteorological variables to their instantaneous distribution in space.

大气的运动规律或许可以用一套偏微分方程来表达，此方程把气象变量的瞬时变化率与其空间的瞬时分布联系在一起。

English passive voice can be rendered into Chinese active voice：

(2) Much remains to be done. While the behavior of temperate latitude cyclones is well represented in current models, the movement of tropical and subtropical disturbances especially into mid-atitude, is not always well-handled.

仍有许多工作需要做。虽然现行的模型极好地描述了中纬度气旋的运动，然而热带和亚热带扰动的运动，尤其是其向中纬度的移动却一直未能很好地掌握。

English passive voice may be rendered into Chinese elliptical sentences.

In Chinese many sentences can be without a subject, which we call elliptical sentences. An example：

(3) Finally, it must be remembered that there is a very strong correlation between the accuracy of forecast and the sufficiency of the data-base from which they are made.

最后，必须记住预报的准确性和制作预报所需数据库的充足性之间有一个极强的关联性。

12.3.3 Ways of Word Class Conversion

Language units can be converted from one class to another in part of speech. The following is an exemplary listing.

From nominal structure to verbal structure:

(4) The conditions required for the convertion of the field weakening emissions of ions from the air around the tip of a lightning rod into return stroke have not been established, and at the current time there is no consensus as to the optimal configuration of lightening rod.

使避雷针尖端周围空气中弱化电场的离子释放并转化成回击的条件目前尚未明确。目前就如何优化配置避雷针也没有形成共识。

English nominal structure remains unchanged in Chinese

(5) All though it was not true in the case of Agnes, loss of life and destruction of property usually are a result of the storm surge, a wave of ocean water generated by the hurricane winds as the storm approaches a coast.

尽管艾格尼斯飓风中的损失数据并不可靠，但是人员的伤亡和财产的毁坏通常是由风暴潮造成的，风暴潮是当风暴抵达海岸时由飓风引起的海水波动。

12.3.4 Tackling Lengthy Sentences

Lengthy sentences are popular in the discourses of meteorology. Translation methods vary in contexts.

Conforming to original order:

(6) Some National Meteorological and Hydrological Services and specialized centers have responsibility for investigating geophysical hazards including volcanic explosions (airborne ash) and tsunamis, and hazardous airborne matter (radionuclides, biological and chemical substances) and acute urban pollution.

一些国家的气象水文部门以及专业中心负责调查地球物理灾害原因，包括火山爆发(空气中的烟灰)和海啸、气载有害物质(放射性核素、生物和化学物质)以及严重的城市污染。

Converting the order of different parts: the translator proceeds from the final part until it ends with the initial part.

(7) The provision of marine meteorological and oceanographic services, to meet the requirement of marine users, is the highest priority for the Marine Meteorology and Oceanography Programme (MMOP), since they contribute substantially to national economies, as well as being essential for the safety of life at sea, as recognized in the International Convention for the Safety of Life at Sea (SOLAS).

正如国际海上人命安全公约(SOLAS 公约)所认可的,海洋气象和海洋学计划(MMOP)为国家经济做出了重要的贡献,在确保海上生命安全方面举足轻重,海洋气象和海洋学计划的最优先考虑是提供海洋气象和海洋服务,以满足海洋用户的需要。

In (7), every word is underlined, but please note there are three different line types: the dot lined part comes at the initial place in English but at the final place in Chinese, the double lined part in the center in both language, the single lined part appears at the end of English but in the very beginning in Chinese. A neatly converted order takes shape.

Reshuffling:

(8) Thanks in large part to advances in geophysical fluid dynamics, the ability to predict with some confidence the paths of hurricanes has led to the establishment of a warning system that, no doubt, has saved numerous lives at sea and in coastal areas.

人类已经建起的预警系统,具有较准确预报飓风来袭路径的能力,这在很大程度上要归功于地球流体力学的发展,该系统无疑已经挽救了海上及沿海地区无数的生命。

Reshuffling means a random rearrangement: the initial part in English appears in the center in Chinese, the central part in English goes to the intial position in Chinese, while the final part in English remains at the same location in Chinese.

12.4 Sample

Haze in China has been a hot topic these years, so our sample will center on this subject.

This kind of air pollutant comes from a variety of natural and manmade sources. Natural sources can include windblown dust, and soot from wildfires. Manmade sources can include motor vehicles, industrial fuel burning, and manufacturing operations.

这种空气污染物来自各种自然和人为来源。天然来源可以包括风沙和野火产生的烟尘。人为来源可以包括机动车辆、工业燃料燃烧和制造作业。

The components that make up haze may have negative effect on people's health especially that of the children and the elderly. Also not excluded are those who have certain diseases such as asthma, allergy, and pneumonia and lung disease. Workers working in the open air have a high risk in their health.

雾霾的组成成分可能对人们的健康有负面影响,特别是对儿童和老人。患有某些疾病如哮喘、过敏、肺炎和肺病的人也不能排除在外。在露天工作的工人有很高的健康风险。

Beijing's pollution crisis appears to have spawned a new fashion trend with dozens of residents seen walking in the smog-ridden streets wearing playfully designed face masks.

北京雾霾危机似乎促使了一个新时尚潮流的产生，现在随处可见市民们带着戏谑的口罩走在被雾霾笼罩的街道上。

Cute monkey, panda and teddy bear designs are all available to those ignoring the authorities' warnings and braving the dangerously high levels of pollution.

政府机构建议尽量少外出的警告全然不能阻挡人们出行：市民们戴着有着可爱小猴、熊猫和泰迪熊等设计的口罩在重污染的空气中勇敢前行。

As the city was recently blanketed by another round of humid still air, the authorities for the first time issued a "red alert", a move that imposes restrictions across much of daily life.

当北京市最近笼罩在又一轮潮湿凝滞的空气中时，北京市政府首次启动空气重污染红色预警，这一举措让人们在日常生活中多处受限。

These two men went for the safety of industrial-quality gas masks, typically used by painters or those dealing in hazardous substances.

这两个男子戴着工业级质量的防毒面具预防有毒空气，一般这种面具都是油漆匠用的，或者是那些暴露在有害物质环境下的人才会用。

12.5 A Glossary of Weather and Climate in English and Chinese

暴风雨 storm, tempest
暴雨 downpour
冰冻 freeze
大气 atmosphere
多云 cloudy
非常冷 freezing
非常冷 freezing cold
风平浪静 dead calm
风势回落了 the wind's dropped
干旱 drought
好像会下雨了 it looks like rain
好像快要下雨 it looks like it's going to rain
季节风 gale
将会有雷暴 we're expecting a thunderstorm
降雪 snowfall

飓风 hurricane
开始下雨了 it's starting to rain
龙卷风 whirlwind
露水 dew
陆风 land wind
浓雾 fog
气候 climate
气温 temperature
气温是零下 it's below freezing
气象学 meteorology
热得像火炉 baking hot
闪电 lightning
湿度 humidity
水龙卷 waterspout
台风 typhoon
太阳出来了 the sun's come out
天空开始明朗了 it's clearing up
天气很好 the weather's fine
天气预报如何? What's the forecast?
天上一点云也没有 there's not a cloud in the sky
天有点阴沉 the sky's overcast
微风 breeze
下冰雹 it's hailing
下大雨 it's pouring with rain
下瓢泼大雨 it's raining cats and dogs
小阳春 Indian summer
旋风 cyclone
雪花 snowflake
阳光被挡住了 the sun's just gone in
阳光充足 sunny
有暴风雨 stormy
有风 windy
有强风 there's a strong wind
有雾 foggy
有阳光 the sun's shining
雨停了 it's stopped raining
预报会下雨 it's forecast to rain
阵风 gust of wind

Chapter 13　Contrast of Sino-Western Cultures and Chinese-English Translation Texts in the Field of Tourism

13.1 What Is Tourism

Tourism is travel for pleasure; also the theory and practice of touring, the business of attracting, accommodating, and entertaining tourists, and the business of operating tours.

The World Tourism Organization defines tourism more generally, in terms which go "beyond the common perception of tourism as being limited to holiday activity only," as people "traveling to and staying in places outside their usual environment for not more than one consecutive year for leisure, business and other purposes."

Tourism can be domestic or international, and international tourism has both incoming and outgoing implications on a country's balance of payments. Today, tourism is a major source of income for many countries, and affects the economy of both the source and host countries, in some cases being of vital importance.

13.2 Cultural Contrast of Tourism in China and the West

13.2.1　Tourism in China

Tourism in China has greatly expanded over the last few decades since the beginning of reform and opening. The emergence of a newly rich middle class and an easing of restrictions on movement by the Chinese authorities are both fueling this travel boom. China has become one of the world's most-watched and hottest inbound and outbound tourist markets. The world is on the cusp (尖端) of a sustained Chinese tourism boom.

In the late 1970s, China started to develop its tourist industry. Major hotel construction programs greatly increased the number of hotels and guest houses, more historic and scenic spots were renovated and opened to tourists, and professional guides and other service personnel were trained.

The expansion of domestic and international airline traffic and other tourist transportation facilities made travel more convenient. Over 250 cities and counties had been opened to foreign visitors by the mid-1980s. Travelers needed only valid visas or residence permits to visit 100 locations; the remaining locales required travel permits from public security departments. In 1985 approximately 1.4 million foreigners visited China, and nearly $1.3 billion was earned from tourism.

Currently, China is the third most visited country in the world. The number of overseas tourists was 55.98 million in 2010. Foreign exchange income was 45.8 billion US dollars, the world's fourth largest in 2010. The number of domestic tourist visits totaled 1.61 billion, with a total income of 777.1 billion yuan. According to the WTO, in 2020, China will become the largest tourist country and among the largest for overseas travel.

China's growing economy is also generating a surge in business travel. In China, the percentage of sales dependent on business travel is higher (38%) as compared to the US (21%) and 28% in the UK, according to the World Travel & Tourism Council's 2013 business travel forecast for the Asia-Pacific region.

13.2.2 Tourism in the West

England's long history and pervasive culture spread worldwide through the English language and colonialism and make England a popular tourist destination, particularly in London.

Heritage cities in England:

Bath: A spa town, famous for its Georgian architecture and crescents, and also for its Roman baths.

Brighton: Brighton is a seaside resort which includes two piers, West Pier and Brighton Pier, and is home to the Royal Pavilion.

Bristol: Brunel's Clifton Suspension Bridge is a famous landmark, and the ship, the SS Great Britain (the largest steam ship at the time when it was built) is another of Brunel's famous constructions.

Cambridge: A famous university town.

Canterbury: Renowned for its cathedral.

Chester: Important Roman and medieval walled city with an amphitheatre and 11th Century Benedictine Abbey, now the Cathedral. Renowned for its covered medieval shop "rows", race course and Chester Zoo.

Dover: A major port with access to the continent. Also well known for its white cliffs, and to a lesser extent for its castle, Dover Castle.

Durham: A famous university town, also renowned for its cathedral and castle.

Exeter: City home to Exeter Cathedral and Rougemont Castle.

Haworth: Where the Brontë sisters lived, is very popular with Japanese tourists, as *Wuthering Heights* has a cult following in Japan.

...

Domestic tourists, and foreign tourists who have specific interests in art, music, history etc. , also visit the following:

Birmingham: A major city, with an orchestra, major exhibition venues and art galleries. Of historical interest for its significant role in the industrial revolution, the childhood home and inspiration of Tolkien, noted for its shopping and boasting the longest stretch of nightclubs in England.

Hadrian's Wall: The Roman wall built in Northumberland by order of the Emperor Hadrian.

Herefordshire: A cathedral city, famous for the chained library in the cathedral, and the Mappa Mundi.

...

Tourism in the United States is a large industry that serves millions of international and domestic tourists yearly. Tourists visit the US to see natural wonders, cities, historic landmarks, and entertainment venues. Americans seek similar attractions, as well as recreation and vacation areas.

Tourism in the United States grew rapidly in the form of urban tourism during the late nineteenth and early twentieth centuries. Tourists spend more money in the United States than any other country, while the US attracting the second-highest number of tourists after France. The discrepancy may be explained by longer stays in the US.

The rise of urban tourism in the United States during the late nineteenth and early twentieth centuries represented a major cultural transformation concerning urban space, leisure natural activity and as an industry. Although travel agents and package tours did not exist until the 1870s and 1880s, entrepreneurs of various sorts from hotel keepers and agents for railroad lines to artists and writers recognized the profit to be gained from the prospering tourism industry. The rise of locomotive steam-powered trains during the 1800s enabled tourists to travel more easily and quickly.

New York, Chicago, Boston, Philadelphia, Washington, D. C. , and San Francisco, all major US cities, attracted a large number of tourists by the 1890s. New York's population grew from 300,000 in 1840 to 800,000 in 1850. Chicago experienced a dramatic increase from 4,000 residents in 1840 to 300,000 by 1870.

Dictionaries first included the word *tourist* sometime in 1800, when it referred to those going to Europe or making a round trip of natural wonders in New York and New England.

13.3 Chinese-English Translation Texts in the Field of Tourism

13.3.1 Cultural Transplantation in Scenary Spot Introduction

Cultural transplantation means transferring what is specific in the source culture into the target culture, and in so doing it can enrich the cultural connotation of the target culture and help readers to better understand the conveyed notion.

The so-called red tourism aims to introduce the contemporary Chinese history to people inside and outside China. Cultural transplantation occurs in the translation of scenary plot introduction, a temporal transplantation to people inside China, a temporal and spatial transplantation to those outside China. Let's see (1) and (2).

(1) 轰轰烈烈的大革命运动,点燃了中国革命的希望。

The full-scale Great Revolution kindled the hope of the Chinese Revolution.

(2) 两军会师,形成了中国红军的主力部队,增强了井冈山根据地的革命武装力量,使根据地的各项建设有了坚强的后盾。

The combination of the two armies formed the principal force of the Chinese Red Army, strengthened the revolutionary military power and provided a powerful backing for various development in the base area.

The above two examples contain some culturally-loaded words such as 大革命运动, 中国革命, 中国红军 and 根据地, demonstrating linguistic, social and cultural features of the Chinese language. Cultural transplantation is enacted in translating them into *the full-scale Great Revolution*, *the Chinese Revolution*, *the Chinese Red Army* and *the base area*. The source flavor of red culture is retained and in turn delivered to readers in English.

Notes, very often footnotes or in-text notes, can be added to supplement cultural connotations in the target language. Here are examples:

(3) 毛泽东适时提出"以乡村为中心"的思想,中国革命开始走向胜利的起点。

Mao Zedong, when the time was ripe, put forward the idea of "taking the rural areas as the center", which was the starting point of the Chinese Revolution.

(4) 您已进入国家5A级旅游风景区井冈山革命烈士陵园。

You have entered the national 5A travelling scenic spot — Jinggangshan Cemetery of Revolutionary Martyrs.

In (3) and (4), 以乡村为中心 and 5A may not be familiar to readers outside China, and their explanation requires some space, so adding notes can be a desirable solution:

The thought of "taking the rural areas as the center" is a great decision made by the CPC after they studied and analyzed the situation at that time. It made good and complete use of a large number of peasants and their urge for the revolution and vast rural area as lead in the Chinese Revolution victory.

5A class tourism scenic area represents a world-class boutique tourist scenic grade. The People's Republic of China tourism scenic quality level is divided into five levels, a descending scale of 5A, 4A, 3A, 2A, A.

13.3.2 Deleting Superfluous Information in the Source Language of Chinese

The Chinese language, especially in literary or quasi-literary texts, uses a lot of beautifully polished descriptions. Tourism spot introductions are quasi-literary texts, in which many four-character idioms are used, which, if literally translated, will seem superfuluous to English readers. Such being the case, a liberal translation is the proper way out: the translator can summarize what is conveyed by superfluous words and rephrase them into simple and logically-guided words. Here are some examples:

(6) 辽阔无垠，绿波荡漾，野花盛开的坝上天然草原，与湖光山影，水天一色的“塞外江南”南北呼应；巍峨隽秀，翠嶂密蔽，层林尽染的原始林区，与泉水潺潺，风光秀丽的温泉依依相存。既有早更新世古人类遗址，又有华夏人文始祖创业的古战场。风格独特，景观各异，有天然质朴之风光，是旅游避暑之佳所。

There are mountains and plateaus scattered with rivers and lakes in the city of Zhangjiakou. The prairies stretch over most part of the city, dotted with ancient ruins and battlefields. A variety of holiday resorts and scenic spots are readily available to tourists from home and abroad. For instance, the vast Bashang Grassland, the marvelous primitive forest and the wonderful hot springs.

In the target language, all the four-character idioms are replaced by a descriptive narration initiated by *there are*.

Two more examples below are more compact:

(7) 潘溪度假村青山环抱，流水潺潺，万松挺拔，繁花似锦，秀美幽静，空气清新，景色十分宜人。

Panxi holiday resort provides an excellent environment for tourists with hills, lakes, pines, and flowers all round, captivating you by its beautiful scenery, tranquility, and fresh air.

In (7), 青山环抱，流水潺潺，万松挺拔，繁花似锦 are replaced with hills, lakes, pines and flowers, one word for one four-character idiom.

(8) 太姥山坐落于东海之滨，山海相依，既是山的海岸又是海的山城，水光山色，互为衬托，构成“山海大观”的景观特色。传说东海神仙每年都会在此山聚会，因此又有“海上仙都”之美誉。它以石奇、洞异、峰险、雾多“四绝”而闻名遐迩。古人赞曰：“太姥无俗石，个个似神工。随人意所识，万象在胸中。”

Taimu Mountain is located in the coast of the East China Sea. The landscape can be seen not only as the seashore of the mountains but the mountain city of the sea, and that the Mountain and the Sea set each other off forms a unique landscape. In legend, the gods living in the East China Sea will get together every year in Taimu Mountain so that the Mountain gets the name of "the City of Gods in the Sea." The Mountain is also famous for the peculiar stones, the singular caves, the perilous peaks and heavy fogs, so it is spoken highly of by the ancients: "There are no common stones but the ones of God's work, whose forms you can imagine with your unlimited ideas."

In (8), the rhymed lines 太姥无俗石，个个似神工，随人意所识，万象在胸中 are

translated into unrhymed prose lines, seeming less aesthetic, but plain and logical.

Sometimes arrangements have to be made to make the target language meet the thinking mode of its readers. Let's see (9):

(9) 在历史的长河中,这座古衙的存在,充分体现了雍干时期的建筑风貌,对古城保定乃至河北历史、建筑等领域文化内涵的补充,起了举足轻重的作用,拥有珍贵的文物价值。

In the course of history, the ancient bureau, with the architectural style of the Qing period, has great historical and cultural value. It plays a decisive role in completing the cultural implication in the domain of history and architecture of Baoding city and even Hebei province.

The source language goes along a spiral route and arrives at its theme at the end of the paragraph when it states ... *has great historical and cultural value*. In translation the supplementary words are presented at the end of the paragraph.

13.3.3 Supplementing Cultural Background Information

Contrary to the practice introduced above, the reverse tact is to supplement some cultural background information so that the target language is more understandable.

(10) 鲁迅纪念馆对外开放场所包括鲁迅故居、百草园、三味书屋。

Open to visitors are Lu Xun's Former Residence, including his Ancestral Residence, Baicao Garden, a waste vegetable plot that made a paradise for little Lu Xun, and Sanwei Study (literally three-flavor study), Shaoxing's most widely known and influential private school in those days where young Lu Xun studied classics for about five years.

In (10), 鲁迅故居, 百草园, 三味书屋 carry too little information when translated word for word into English. The translator explained them one by one as shown above.

In (11), an in-text explanation is inserted to facilitate understanding. Very often, 观音 or 观世音 in Chinese tourist spot introduction is often transliterated into *Guanyin* or *Guanshiyin* rather than the Sanskrit Avalokiteśvara. Translieration is indirect and flouts the principle of name-translating which Confucius advocated in《谷梁传 · 桓公二年》as "名从主人" (names should be said as their owners are called).

(11) 宫内既供黄大仙,又奉观世音……

In the Taoist temple, people enshrine and worship Wong Tai Sin (an immortal good at alchemy and medicine) and Avalokiteśvara (the Goddess of Mercy).

In (12) below, 济公 is a familiar Buddhist monk who has many supernatural powers in punishing the wicked and helping the wretched, but this image is exotic to English readers, hence licensing the necessity of an explanation — the contrastive insertion of *Robin Hood in China* is sufficient.

(12) 济公劫富济贫，深受穷困人民爱戴。

Jigong, Robin Hood in China, robbed the rich and helped the poor.

13.4 Samples

The samples quoted below are composed of C-E translation of Chinese scenic spots and E-C translation of Russian and American ones.

这块岩石构成的图形恰似“圣门”，也就是人类神圣的生命之门。它本身具有“生”的象征。传统的船工在此举行祭拜仪式——圣门祭母，是生殖图腾崇拜的一种古老习俗。这种祭拜目的在于求佑平安，希望无灾无难，体现了一种原始民俗，具有深厚的人文内涵。

This graph formed by rocks looks like “Saint Gate”, which is the sacred door of life for humans. It has its own symbol of life. Traditionally, boatmen held sacrificial ceremonies to worship their mothers at Saint Gate that is reproductive totem worship of an ancient custom. Its purpose is to seek peace and safety. It embodies a primitive folk custom, and it has a profound humanistic content.

黄河两岸农家生活的原生态，黄河岸边无数普通农家生活的真实展现。这里陈列了农家必需的生产工具与生活用品，如纺花机、织布机、切草刀等，体现着黄河人家生活的简单、艰辛和乐观，既可满足中老年游客的怀旧情感，又可使年轻人接受传统教育。

This exhibition shows the original ecosystem of the farm life of the common people along the Yellow River. Here you can see the necessary tools of production and daily necessities, such as spinning wheels, weaving machines, grass-cutting knives etc., which embody the simplicity, hardship and optimism of the life of the local people. It can not only meet the nostalgic feelings of the elderly tourists, but also enable young people to accept the traditional education.

吞吐烟云的闯王寨，是 1636 年李自成进攻中原受挫后的屯兵之地。他带领余部五十余人在此休养生息后东山再起。闯王寨峰峦叠嶂，云霞缭绕，视野开阔，极目远眺，黄河两岸上下全在视野之中，黄河大碛土金碛上骇浪惊天，视听胜于近前。寨前峡谷幽静，清泉不竭，登古寨却只有一条路，可谓一夫当关，万夫莫开。

Chuangwang Stockaded Village is the place where Li Zicheng stationed his troops in 1636 after he failed in attacking the Central Plains. He led the remaining 50 soldiers of his army to recuperate before a comeback. There are many mountains here with ridges and peaks rising one after another, and rosy clouds flying. It has a wide field of vision. As far as the eye could see all was the panoramic view of the Yellow River. You can see the great moraines in the Yellow River. There are springs here with inexhaustible water. There is only one way into the Village. It is just like an old Chinese saying: If one man guards the pass, ten thousand cannot get through.

St. Petersburg. The very name brings to mind some of Russia's greatest poets, writers and composers: Pushkin, Dostoevsky, Tchaikovsky. The 19th century was a golden age for St. Petersburg's wealthy classes. It was a world of ballets and balls, of art and literature, of tea and caviar.

圣彼得堡，只要提到这个名字就让人想起那些俄国最伟大的诗人、作家以及作曲家：普希金、陀思妥耶夫斯基、柴可夫斯基。19 世纪对圣彼得堡的富有阶级来说是段黄金岁月。那是一个充满了芭蕾舞和舞会、艺术和文学、茶和鱼子酱的世界。

St. Petersburg had become Petrograd in 1914. People wanted a Russian name for their city. Ten years later, the city's name changed again, this time to Leningrad. Then in 1991, Leningraders voted to restore the city's original name. Some people opposed the name change altogether. Others thought it was just too soon. Old, run-down Soviet Leningrad, they said, was not the St. Petersburg of 19th-century literature.

圣彼得堡在 1914 年变成彼得格勒。人们想为这个城市取个俄国名字。十年之后，这个城市的名字又改了，这一次叫做列宁格勒。然后在 1991 年，列宁格勒的居民投票恢复了此城最初的名字。有些人彻底反对改名字，有些人认为名字改得太快了。他们说老旧的苏维埃列宁格勒已不再是 19 世纪的圣彼得堡了。

For most of us, Hawaii begins to weave her spell with some little glimmer of awareness. Golden beaches and golden people. Sun, sand, sea, and surf... And somewhere between the blue skies and the palm trees... We're hooked.

对于大部分人来说，那些星星点点的关于夏威夷的印象，足以让我们沉浸于她的魅力。金色的海滩，金色的人们。阳光、沙子、大海、浪花……在蓝天和棕榈树之间，我们流连忘返。

The Hawaiian Islands are one of the most beautiful places on earth. The weather is friendly. The temperature ranges from 60—90 degrees all year long. It's a little warmer in summer, and a little cooler in winter, but every day is a beach day for somebody.

夏威夷岛是世界上最美丽的地方之一。这里天气宜人，气温整年在华氏 60—90 度之间变化。夏天稍暖，冬天稍凉，但对于某些人来说每天都是晒太阳的好日子。

13.5 A Glossary of Tourism in English and Chinese

淡季 off season, off-peak season
地方旅游组织 local tourist organization
地陪，地方导游 local guide
国际旅游 international tourism

国家级历史文化名城 state-list famous historical and cultural cities
会多种语言的导游 multilingual guide
领队，团长 tour leader
旅费 travelling expense
旅行计划 itinerary
旅游安排 tour arrangement
旅游地图 tourist map
旅游点 tourist spots
旅游记者 travel journalist
旅游界 tourism circles
旅游局 Tourist Administration
旅游俱乐部 touring club
旅游路线 tour route
旅游目的地 tourist destination
旅游团目录 tour catalog
旅游团陪同 tour escort/conductor/director
旅游委员会 tourist council
旅游小册子 tour brochure
旅游协会 tourist association
旅游业 travel industry
旅游指南 guide book
旅游组织 tourist organization
区域旅游组织 regional tourist organization
省旅游局 Provincial Tourism Administration
世界旅游日 World Tourism Day
世界旅游组织 World Tourism Organization
市旅游局 Municipal Tourism Administration
旺季 on season，peak season
游客 tourist
游览 sightseeing

Chapter 14 Contrast of Sino-Western Cultures and Chinese-English Translation Texts in the Field of Trade

14.1 What Is Trade

Trade involves the transfer of the ownership of goods or services from one person or entity to another in exchange for other goods or services or for money.

The original form of trade, barter, saw the direct exchange of goods and services for other goods and services. Barter is trading things without the use of money. Later one side of the barter started to involve precious metals, which gained symbolic as well as practical importance. Modern traders generally negotiate through a medium of exchange, such as money. As a result, buying can be separated from selling, or earning. The invention of money (and later credit, paper money and non-physical money) greatly simplified and promoted trade. Trade between two traders is called bilateral trade, while trade between more than two traders is called multilateral trade.

14.2 Cultural Contrast of Trade in China and the West

14.2.1 Trade in China

In the long history of the so-called feudal society, trade or commerce was looked down upon and considered an inferior occupation. The off-springs of businessmen were not allowed to attend the imperial examination or seek positions in the government organs.

Since China's opening and reform in the late 1970s, trade has been a very significant factor of economy in China. The drive to modernize the economy that began in 1978 required a sharp acceleration in commodity flows and greatly improved efficiency in economic transactions.

In the ensuing years economic reforms were adopted by the government to develop a socialist market economy. This type of economy combined central planning with market mechanisms. The changes resulted in the decentralization and expansion of domestic and foreign trade institutions, as well as a greatly enlarged role for free markets in the distribution of goods, and a prominent role for foreign trade and investment in economic development.

In 2014 China surpassed the United States as the largest trading nation in the world. Now China plays a vital role in international trade, and has increasingly engaged in trade organizations and treaties in recent years.

China became a member of the World Trade Organization in 2001. China also has free trade agreements with several nations, including China-Australia Free Trade Agreement, China-South Korea Free Trade Agreement, ASEAN-China Free Trade Area.

14.2.2 Trade in the West

The World Trade Organization (WTO) is an intergovernmental organization which regulates international trade. The WTO deals with regulation of trade between participating countries by providing a framework for negotiating trade agreements and a dispute resolution process aimed at enforcing participants' adherence to WTO agreements, which are signed by representatives of member governments and ratified by their parliaments. Most of the issues that the WTO focuses on derive from previous trade negotiations, especially from the Uruguay Round (1986—1994).

The WTO is attempting to complete negotiations on the Doha Development Round, which was launched in 2001 with an explicit focus on developing countries. As of June 2012, the future of the Doha Round remained uncertain: the work programme lists 21 subjects in which the original deadline of 1 January 2005 was missed, and the round is still incomplete. The conflict between free trade on industrial goods and services but retention of protectionism on farm subsidies to domestic agricultural sector (requested by developed countries) and the substantiation of fair trade on agricultural products (requested by developing countries) remain the major obstacles. This impasse (僵局) has made it impossible to launch new WTO negotiations beyond the Doha Development Round. As a result, there have been an increasing number of bilateral free trade agreements between governments. As of July 2012, there were various negotiation groups in the WTO system for the current agricultural trade negotiation which is in the condition of stalemate.

In most countries including the UK and the USA, trade represents a significant share of gross domestic product (GDP). While international trade has been present throughout much of history, its economic, social, and political importance has been on the rise in recent centuries. It is the presupposition of international trade that a sufficient level of geopolitical peace and stability are prevailing in order to allow for the peaceful exchange of trade and commerce to take place between nations.

The UK has been a great power in international trade. Its deficit on trade in goods and services widened by £0.7 billion to £3.7 billion in February 2017 from an upwardly revised £3.0 billion in January. Imports increased in the month by £0.3 billion to a new record of £52.1 billion, due to an increase in purchases of goods from the EU. Exports decreased by £0. 4 billion to £48. 5 billion, led by a decrease in exports of trade in services of £0. 3 billion.

The United States has trade relations with many other countries. Within that, the trade with Europe and Asia is predominant. To fulfill the demands of the industrial sector, the country has to import mineral oil and iron ore on a large scale. Machinery, cotton yarn, toys, mineral oil, lubricants, steel, tea, sugar, coffee, and many more items are traded. The country's export list includes food grains like wheat, corn, and soybean. Aeroplane, cars, computers, paper, and machine tools are required for different industries. In 2016 United States current account balance was −469. 4 billion US dollars.

14.3 Chinese-English Translation Texts in the Field of Trade

Translation in the field of trade is more than diversified. It requires the space of a whole book to cover all subfields of trade. So we shall confine our contrast to commercial ads as an example which, when substantially stretched, can reflect the differences in all stages of trade in the languages of Chinese and English.

14.3.1 Resorting to Linguistic Deviations

Commercial ads resort to linguistic deviations in order to attract the attention of ad recipients. When two languages are involved and one language, the source, makes use of deviations in grammar or semantics or pragmatics, the other language, the target, will have to respond to it. If the response is made at the same level, that is, grammar deviation for grammar deviation, and semantics deviation for semantics deviation, and so on, so much the better. Very often, due to the differences in language typology, cross correspondences of deviations have to be made with the source language deviating at one level and the target language deviating at another. Let's see examples.

The advertising slogan of Benz car of S-Class is:

(1) This is The car.

The article *the* should not be capitalized unless in the initial location of a sentence, but in (1) it is, obviously deviating from the grammar norm. In translating into Chinese which uses no articles but demonstrative pronouns 这,那,这些 and 那些, the deviation has to be attached to some other word or in some other form. It is well done when (1) is translated into (2):

(2) 这才是車!

The deviation falls on the classical Chinese character 車 which stands out as a contrast in the mainland of China where simplified Chinese characters are used. A direct clue for the deviation is that 这 is the simplified form rather than the unsimplied 這. It is ridiculous to mix up the use of simplified and unsimplied Chinese characters. Yes, this is what is expected of the effect. A correspondence of deviation, though not at the same level. One more example:

(3) Apple thinks different.

Apple here refers to some electronic device, so it cannot think as human beings or animals do. When apple and think co-occur in the same context, a deviation arises which we call personification or metaphorical use. A corresponding figurative use is of course feasible in Chinese, but things can be better done than that as can be shown in (4):

(4) 苹果电脑,非同凡"想"。

In (4) 想 is homophonous with 响, deviating in semantic coherence, hence a good match with that in (3), though not the same type.

14.3.2 Marking the Differences in Culture

The Chinese culture and the English culture differ diametrically as their locations of attachment are far apart in the east hemisphere and the west respectively. Cultural differences permeate in the creation and use of commercial ads as in any other genre of language use. Here are some fields where differences arise.

1. Focus or Non-focus

English sentences have syntactic and/or semantic focuses; once a focus is determined it cannot be ignored. But in Chinese, more than one focus is allowed in a sentence. Let's compare:

(5) 输入千言万语,奏出一片深情(文字处理机)

This word processor plays a tune of deep feeling whenever you are typing.

Here, 输入 is a literal statement and 奏出 is a metaphorical comparison between music playing and machine use. Juxtoposition deprives the clauses of a focus. But its English counterpart has a unique focus in syntax and semantics, subordinating the non-focus perspective by the use of *whenever*.

2. Differences in Value

Value is the substantial part of culture, most stable and determining among all forming parts in culture, including material culture, system culture and notional culture. Notional culture has value as its core.

(6) 雀巢咖啡伴侣,默默奉献,为香浓加分!(雀巢公司广告)

Coffee's perfect mate

The Chinese version in (6) represents the Chinese people's valued conception of collectivism (集体主义) which stresses silent contribution without claiming a legal repay. The English version uses a distinct image of *mate*, highlighting equality among people, metaphorically mapped to the making of coffee out of two ingredients, the coffee powder and its mate.

(7) 衣食住行，有龙则灵（龙卡广告语）

Your everyday life is very busy; our Long Card can make it easy.

The Chinese people claim themselves to be descendents of the dragon, so the legendary animal is the national totem of the Chinese people. However, English-speaking people have a strong negative opinion for dragon. To avoid the unwanted awkwardness, dragon is transliterated into *Long*.

14.3.3 Inclinations for Passive or Active

As we have observed somewhere in the previous chapters, English has an inclination for using the passive voice while Chinese for the active voice. In commercial ads, the contrast holds true as well. Let's see examples.

(8) Payment shall be effected within seven days after receipt of the shipping documents stipulated under Clause 10 of this Contract.

货款须在收到本合同第 10 条规定的装运单据后的 7 天内支付。

In (8) the passive voice *be effected* is echoed by the active 支付. Contrasts in (9) are marked by the underlined corresponding words as above.

(9) It is strictly understood that the Sellers cannot be held responsible for non-delivery or delayed delivery of the goods ordered if the situation is caused by force majeure, war, rebellion, fire, strike, new levies imposed by government, mistakes in telegrams, inability of or refusal by the manufacturers to fulfill this contract or any other causes beyond Seller's control.

合同严格明确如果卖方不能够交货或者迟延交货是由不可抗力、战争、叛乱、火灾、罢工、政府新征税收、电报错误、生产商不能或拒绝履行合同，或其它不受卖方控制的原因所导致的，卖方不承担责任。

14.4 Samples

The samples quoted below are frequently used contract clauses, whose sentence patterns can facilitate reading or translating when familiarized.

At the request of Party B, Party A agrees to send technicians to assist Party B to install the equipment.

应乙方要求，甲方同意派遣技术人员帮助乙方安装设备。

This Contract shall be governed by and construed in accordance with the laws of China.

本合同受中国法律管辖，并按中国法律解释。

The Employer may object to and require the Contractor to replace forthwith any of its authorized representatives who is incompetent.

雇主认为承包人委派的授权代表不合格时，可以反对并要求立即撤换。

The Chairperson may convene an interim meeting based on a proposal made by one-third of the total number of directors.

董事长可以根据董事会过1/3董事的提议而召集临时董事会议。

In case one party desires to sell or assign all or part of its investment subscribed, the other party shall have the preemptive right.

如一方欲出售或转让其投资之全部或部分，另一方有优先购买权。

In processing transactions, the manufacturers shall never have title either to the materials or the finished products.

加工贸易中，厂方无论是对原料还是成品都无所有权。

The term "Effective date" means the date on which this Agreement is duly executed by the parties hereto.

"生效期"指双方合同签字的日期。

This Contract shall be written in English in four copies. Each party shall keep two copies.

本合同应以英文写成，一式四份，双方各持两份。

The following documents shall be deemed to form and be read and construed as an integral part of this Contract.

下列文件应被认为、读作、解释为本合同的组成部分。

This Contract can only be altered, amended or supplemented in accordance with documents signed and sealed by authorized representatives of both parties.

本合同只能按照双方授权代表签名盖章的文件进行修改或增补。

All activities of ABC Co. shall be governed by the laws, decrees and pertinent rules and regulations of China.

ABC公司的一切活动必须受中国的法律、法令和有关规章条例的管辖。

Party B is hereby appointed by Party A as its exclusive sales agent in Singapore.

乙方被甲方委托为在新加坡的独家销售代理商。

Licensee may terminate this Contract 90 days after a written notice thereof is sent to Licensor upon the happening of one of the following events:

当有下列事件之一发生，被许可人提前 90 天向许可人发送书面通知后，可以终止合同：

1. Licensor becomes insolvent or a liquidator of Licensor is appointed;
   许可人无力偿付债务或其破产清算人已被指定；
2. The patent described in Article 2 is not issued within 30 days from signing this Contract;
   第二条规定的专利未在签约后 30 天之内发布；
3. Licensor fails to perform its obligations under this Contract.
   许可人未能履行其合同义务。

In consideration of the payment to be made by Party A to Party B, Party B hereby covenants with Party A to complete the building in conformity with the provisions of the Contract.

乙方特此立约向甲方保证按合同规定完成工程建设，以取得甲方所付的报酬。

14.5 A Glossary of Trade in English and Chinese

承兑，接受 acceptance
承兑人 acceptor
承兑信用证 acceptance letter of credit (acceptance L/C)
承兑行 accepting bank
承运货物收据 cargo receipt
船方负担装卸费 berth terms
船龄证明书 certificate of age of vessel
代理商 agent
倒签提单 ante-dated bill of lading (ante-dated B/L)
递盘 bid
电报证实书 cable confirmation
电挂 cable address (C/A)
电开信用证 cable credit
订货时付款 cash in order (C. I. O)
对背信用证 back to back letter of credit (back to back L/C)
防止延迟 avoidance of delay
付款兑现 available by payment
购货发盘 buying offer
海运提单 bill of lading (B/L)

航空货运单 air waybill
航空运输货物战争险 air transportation cargo war risks
航空运输险 air transportation risks
航空运输一切险 air transportation all risks
回购 buy back
汇票 bill of exchange
货物舱单 cargo manifest
寄单证明 certificate for dispatch of documents
寄售协议 agreement of consignment
寄样证明 certificate for dispatch of shipment samples
加速贸易付款 accelerate trade payment (ATP)
简电本 brief cable
交货付款 cash on delivery (C. O. D)
交易磋商 business negotiation
解约日 canceling date
空白背书 blank endorsement
款项让渡 assignment of proceed
捆包装 bale packing
来件装配 assembling with customer's parts
冷藏货物运输一切险 all risks for shipment of frozen products
买方远期信用证 buyer's usance credit
买期保值 buying hedging
拍卖 auction
拍卖人 auctioneer
凭单付款 cash against documents
燃油附加费 bunker adjustment factor (BAF)
散装货物 bulk cargo, cargo in bulk
善意持有人 bona fide holder
实际交货 actual delivery
实际全损 actual total loss
随订单付现 cash with order (C. W. O)
套合一致的单证 aligned document system
提单货量 bill of lading weight
通知行 advising bank
投保声明的回执 acknowledgement of insurance declaration
投标保证金,投标押金 bid bond
托收汇票 bill for collection (B/C)
托运单 booking note

违反担保或违反随附条件 breach of warranty
违反合同 breach of contract
违反无名条款 breach of innominate terms
违反中间性条款 breach of intermediate terms
现金折扣 cash discount
信用卡 credit card
议付兑现 available by negotiation
易货贸易 barter trade
银行保证函 bank guarantee
银行承兑汇票 banker's acceptance bill
银行承兑信用证 banker's acceptance letter of credit (banker's acceptance L/C)
银行费用 banking charges
银行支票 banker's cheque
英国(工业)标准 British Standard (BS)
由买方决定 at buyer's option
由卖方决定 at seller's option
预付货款 advanced payment
预付现款 cash in advance (C. I. A)
预借提单 advanced bill of lading (advanced B/L)
预支信用证 anticipatory letter of credit (anticipatory L/C)
招标 call for tender
仲裁程序 arbitration procedure
仲裁申请 arbitration application
仲裁条款 arbitration clause
仲裁协议 arbitration agreement
自动循环信用证 automatic revolving L/C

Chapter 15 Contrast of Sino-Western Cultures and Chinese-English Translation Texts in the Field of Flora and Fauna

15.1 What Are Flora and Fauna

Flora is the plant life occurring in a particular region or time, generally the naturally occurring or indigenous plant life. The corresponding term for animal life is fauna.

Flora, fauna and other forms of life such as fungi are collectively referred to as biota (一时代或一地区的动植物). Sometimes bacteria and fungi are also referred to as flora, as in the terms gut flora(肠道菌群) or skin flora(皮肤菌群).

Fauna is all of the animal life of any particular region or time. Fauna comes from the Latin names *Fauna*, a Roman goddess of earth and fertility, the Roman god *Faunus*, and the related forest spirits called *Fauns*. All three words are cognates of the name of the Greek god Pan, and panis is the Greek equivalent of fauna. Fauna is also the word for a book that catalogues the animals in such a manner. The term was first used by Linnaeus in the title of his 1745 work *Fauna Suecica*(《瑞典动物志》).

15.2 Cultural Contrast of Flora and Fauna in China and the West

15.2.1 Flora and Fauna in China

China is one of the countries with the greatest diversity of wildlife in the world. There are more than 6,266 species of vertebrates, 10 percent of the world's total. Among them 2,404 are terrestrials and 3,862 fishes. Wild animals peculiar to China includes such well-known rare animals as panda, golden-haired monkey, South China tiger, brown-eared pheasant(野鸡), red-crowned crane, crested ibis(朱鹭), white-flag dolphin and Chinese alligator(短吻鳄), totaling more than 100 species. The black-and-white-haired giant panda weighs on average 135 kg and lives on tender bamboo leaves and bamboo shoots. Because it is extremely rare—just over 1,000 are left at present — it has become the symbol of the world's protected wild animals. The red-crowned crane, 1.2 m tall on average, is covered with white feathers, and a distinctive patch of exposed red skin tops its head, which is regarded as the symbol of longevity in East Asia. The white-flag dolphin is one of only two species of fresh water whales in the world. In 1980, a male white-flag dolphin was caught for the first time in the Yangtze River, which aroused great interest among dolphin researchers worldwide.

China is also one of the countries with the most abundant plant life in the world. There are more than 32,000 species of higher plants, and almost all the major plants that grow in the northern hemisphere's frigid, temperate and tropical zones are found in China. In addition, there are more than 7,000 species of woody plants, including 2,800-odd tree species. The metasequoia(水杉), Chinese cypress, Cathay silver fir, China fir, golden larch(落叶松), Taiwan fir, Fujian cypress, dove-tree, eucommia(杜仲) and camplotheca acuminate(喜树) are found only in China. The metasequoia, a tall species of arbor(乔木), is considered to be one of the oldest and rarest plants in the world. The golden larch, one of only five species of rare garden trees in the world, grows in the mountainous areas in the Yangtze River valley. Its coin-shaped leaves on short branches are green in spring and summer, turning yellow in autumn. China is home to more than 2,000 species of edible plants and over 3,000 species of medicinal plants. Ginseng from the Changbai Mountains, safflowers(藏红花) from Tibet, Chinese wolfberry(枸杞) from Ningxia and notoginseng (三七) from Yunnan and Guizhou are particularly well-known Chinese herbal medicines. There is a wide variety of flowering plants. A flower indigenous to China, the peony, known as the "king of flowers," characterized by large blossoms, multiple petals and bright colors, is treasured as one of the country's national flowers.

Chinese herbology(草药学) is the theory of traditional Chinese herbal therapy, which accounts for the majority of treatments in traditional Chinese medicine (TCM).

Chinese herbs have been used for centuries. Among the earliest literature are lists of prescriptions for specific ailments, exemplified by the manuscript *Recipes for 52 Ailments* (《五十二病方》), found in the Mawangdui tombs in Changsha which were sealed before 168 BC.

15.2.2 Flora and Fauna in the West

Many of Europe's flowering plants are similar to those in North America, belonging to many of the same genera(属) but to different species(种). Some of the most common North American flowering plants have cousins in Europe, but their location varies according to their latitude(纬度) and altitude(海拔).

The most important factor determining the location of plants is climate. The continent of Europe ranges from the coastal areas on the northern shores of the Mediterranean Sea and Black Sea to the Arctic Ocean north of the Scandinavian Peninsula. Although most of Europe is in the temperate climate zone, the areas that border the Mediterranean Sea are nearly all frost-free.

With its mild climate and varied soils, the United Kingdom has a diverse pattern of natural vegetation. Originally, oak forests probably covered the lowland, except for the fens(沼泽地带) and marsh areas, while pine forests and patches of moorland covered the higher or sandy ground. Over the centuries, much of the forest area, especially on the lowlands, was cleared for cultivation. Today only about 9% of the total surface is wooded. Fairly extensive forests remain in east and north Scotland and in southeast England. Oak, elm, ash, and beech are the most common trees in England. Pine and birch are most common in Scotland. Almost all the lowland outside the industrial centers is farmland, with a varied seminatural vegetation of grasses and flowering plants. Wild vegetation consists of the natural flora of woods, fens and marshes, cliffs, chalk downs(白垩山丘), and mountain slopes, the most widespread being the heather, grasses, gorse(金雀花), and bracken(欧洲蕨) of the moorlands.

The fauna is similar to that of northwestern continental Europe, although there are fewer species. Some of the larger mammals—wolf, bear, boar, and reindeer—are extinct, but red and roe deer are protected for sport. Common smaller mammals are foxes, hares, hedgehogs, rabbits, weasels, stoats(白鼬), shrews(鼩鼱), rats, and mice; otters(水獭) are found in many rivers, and seals frequently appear along the coast. There are few reptiles and amphibians. Roughly 230 species of birds reside in the United Kingdom, and another 200 are migratory. Most numerous are the chaffinch(花鸡), blackbird, sparrow, and starling(欧椋鸟). The number of large birds is declining, however, except for game birds—pheasant, partridge, and red grouse (松鸡)—which are protected. With the reclamation of the marshlands, waterfowl are moving to the many bird sanctuaries. The rivers and lakes abound in salmon, trout, perch, pike, roach, dace, and grayling. There are more than 21,000 species of insects.

In the United States at least 7,000 species and subspecies of indigenous US flora have been categorized. The eastern forests contain a mixture of softwoods and hardwoods that includes pine, oak, maple, spruce, beech, birch, hemlock, walnut, gum, and hickory. The central hardwood forest, which originally stretched unbroken from Cape Cod to Texas and northwest to Minnesota — still an important timber source — supports oak, hickory, ash, maple, and walnut. Pine, hickory, tupelo, pecan, gum, birch, and sycamore are found in the southern forest that stretches along the Gulf Coast into the eastern half of Texas. The Pacific forest is the most spectacular of all because of its enormous redwoods and Douglas firs. In the southwest are saguaro (giant cactus), yucca, candlewood, and the Joshua tree.

The central grasslands lie in the interior of the continent, where the moisture is not sufficient to support the growth of large forests. The tall grassland or prairie (now almost entirely under cultivation) lies to the east of the 100th meridian(经线). To the west of this line, where rainfall is frequently less than 50 cm per year, is the short grassland. Mesquite

(豆科灌木) grass covers parts of west Texas, southern New Mexico, and Arizona. Short grass may be found in the highlands of the latter two states, while tall grass covers large portions of the coastal regions of Texas and Louisiana and occurs in some parts of Mississippi, Alabama, and Florida. The Pacific grassland includes northern Idaho, the higher plateaus of eastern Washington and Oregon, and the mountain valleys of California.

An estimated 432 species of mammals characterize the animal life of the continental United States. Among the larger game animals are the white-tailed deer, moose(驼鹿), pronghorn antelope(叉角羚), bighorn sheep, mountain goat, black bear, and grizzly bear. The Alaskan brown bear often reaches a weight of 1,200—1,400 pounds. Some 25 important furbearers are common, including the muskrat(麝鼠), red and gray foxes, mink (貂), raccoon (浣熊), beaver, opossum (负鼠), striped skunk (臭鼬), woodchuck, cottontail(白尾灰兔), snowshoe hare, and various squirrels. Human encroachment has transformed the mammalian habitat over the last two centuries. The American buffalo (bison), millions of which once roamed the plains, is now found only on select reserves. Other mammals, such as the elk and gray wolf, have been restricted to much smaller ranges.

Year-round and migratory birds abound. Loons(潜鸟), wild ducks, and wild geese are found in lake country; terns(燕鸥), gulls, sandpipers(鹬), herons(苍鹭), and other seabirds live along the coasts. Wrens(鹪鹩), thrushes(画眉), owls, hummingbirds, sparrows, woodpeckers, swallows, chickadees(山雀), vireos(绿鹃), warblers(啭鸟), and finches(雀类) appear in profusion, along with the robin, common crow, cardinal(主红雀), Baltimore oriole, eastern and western meadowlarks, and various blackbirds. Wild turkey, ruffed grouse(披肩鸡), and ring-necked pheasant (introduced from Europe) are popular game birds.

15.3 Chinese-English Translation Texts in the Field of Flora and Fauna

15.3.1 Cultural Implications of Plants

Attaching symbolic value to plants, flowers, and trees is a phenomenon common to all languages and cultures. In China, the cultivation and appreciation of plants is something that began thousands of years ago. From those times onward, Chinese people had endowed many plants with special significance. Writers, poets and painters have long depicted flowers and trees in their artistic pursuits. Over time, the symbolism of plants has become a complex part of Chinese culture. Historically, plants have also been thought to embody certain spiritual features that have shaped the customs and character of China as a nation.

China is famous as being home to many thousands of varieties of flowers, many of which are cultivated for the personal pleasure of Chinese people. The ten most widely appreciated and culturally significant are peony, Chinese herbaceous peony(芍药), camellia(茶花), azalea(杜鹃花), narcissus(水仙), chrysanthemum, plum blossom, lotus, Chinese flowering crab apple(海棠) and orchid(兰花). Pine and bamboo are also very popular. Many different aspects of plants, flowers and trees are admired, including their shapes, colors, and scents. Furthermore, they are often endowed with spiritual and human attributes. In Chinese, the expression Three Friends in Cold Winter(岁寒三友) refers to pine, bamboo and plum trees. Similarly, the expression Four Men of Honor(四君子) refers to plum, orchid, bamboo and chrysanthemum, and Four Elegancies(四雅) refers to the simple yet graceful orchid, chrysanthemum, narcissus and calamus(菖蒲).

Pine is held in high esteem as one of the Three Friends in Cold Winter because it is evergreen, grows straight and tall, and can endure cold weather with relative ease. People value it as a symbol of integrity, tenacity and uprightness. Confucius once said "Only after it turns winter are we aware of the survival of the pine and cypress."(岁寒，然后知松柏之后凋也。) The famous Tang Dynasty poet Li Bai wrote:

A giant pine grows on Mt Taihua,
Erect and upright over hoar frost and snow;
Reaching the sky tall and strong,
It never bends when wind blows.

(太华生长松，
亭亭凌霜雪。
天与百尺高，
岂为微飙折。
——《赠书侍御黄裳》)

Pine represents a spirit of strength and perseverance, and of maintaining one's integrity regardless of circumstances. Due to the fact that pine trees grow to a great age, they are also a symbol of longevity. In Chinese art pine trees and cranes represent long life. When being sent as greetings to older people on their birthdays, these especially popular couplets are often used:

As auspicious as the unceasing water in the eastern sea. As timeless as the longevity pine of the southern mountain.(福如东海，寿比南山)

A thousand year old crane. An evergreen pine tree.(千年鹤，长青松)

As long living as the pine and cypress. As graceful as an orchid.(寿比松柏，雅如幽兰)

Every branch on a pine tree is over one hundred years. Every fruit of a peach tree is over a thousand years.(松枝逾百岁，桃寿越千年)

Bamboo is depicted in both Three Friends in Cold Winter and Four Men of Honor, and has many rhetorical implications in Chinese culture. Somewhat similar to pine, the fact that it is evergreen, and its stems are strong and hard makes it an apt symbol of integrity, strength and loyalty. In Chinese, the hollow culms(茎) and the nodes of bamboo are homophones for modesty with self-esteem. The worship of bamboo as a form of divine being was recorded in several classical history books, including *The Annual of the Huayang Kingdom* (《华阳国志》, 又名《华阳国记》), which was one of the earliest chronicles of southeast China. It was also mentioned in *The History of the Later Han Dynasty*(《后汉书》).

Chinese history is replete with bamboo aficionados(竹痴), but three of them are particularly worth discussing. The first was Wang Huizhi(王徽之), the fifth of Wang Xizhi's seven sons, the great master of calligraphy in the Jin Dynasty (265—420). One day Wang Huizhi heard of a remarkable variety of bamboo growing at the house of a scholar-official. Going to view it, he became so entranced in its exquisiteness that he did not hear the greetings of the host of the house. Another time, he stayed away from home for some days. So much he did miss his beloved bamboo that he asked to have some planted beside his temporary home. "How could I live without gentleman bamboo?" he asked rhetorically. Ever since then, bamboo came to be commonly referred to as "gentleman bamboo."

The great Song Dynasty poet and food connoisseur(鉴赏家) Su Shi once noted that "To live without meat will only make one thinner, but to live without sight of bamboo, this will make one vulgar."(无肉令人瘦,无竹令人俗。)

Finally, Zheng Banqiao, a prodigiously talented Qing Dynasty artist noted for his writing, painting, and calligraphy not only painted bamboo but also wrote poetry praising its qualities. He boasted that not only had he painted bamboo for over 40 years, he also spent a great deal of time reflecting on its virtues and aesthetic value. In one of his poems, he wrote:

Harsh autumn wind has come to the south,
Sweeping stone and wood furiously.
Among the plants, only bamboo fears not,
Standing erect against the wind for many rounds courageously.
(秋风昨夜渡潇湘,
触石穿林惯作狂,
惟有竹枝浑不怕,
挺然相斗一千场。)

The high degree of esteem in which bamboo is held in Chinese culture is accurately expressed in this poem.

Like bamboo, the plum blossom holds a place in both Three Friends in Cold Winter and Four Men of Honor. The graceful blossom can withstand freezing cold that kills other flowers, and also has a delightful scent. Because it is the earliest blossom to bloom after winter, it stands out among its peers. And like bamboo and pine, the plum blossom also had its legion of fans. Lin Bu, a Song Dynasty hermit who lived at Mt Gushan near the

West Lake in Hangzhou was famous for his love of both plum trees and cranes. An idiom, 梅妻鹤子, literally meaning plum as wife and cranes as children, was actually generated from Lin Bu's way of life, as a metaphor for a lifestyle free of worldly worries. Lin Bu's poem on plum was regarded the most classic in praise of the plant, but there were others who also expressed it artistically, including Lu You in the Southern Song Dynasty, and Wang Mian from the Yuan Dynasty, who both wrote and painted. In poetry, the plum blossom is often praised for its ability to preserve purity and charm, and help lead an honorable life.

The character 梅 (plum) has over time been incorporated into the names of people, places, books, music and art forms. The name of a noted Qing Dynasty scholar, Chen Mengmei(陈梦梅), means dreaming of plum. A scholar of the Southern Song, Shi Dazu (史达祖), gave himself the additional name of "plum creek" (号梅溪).

Orchid is admired for its charming fragrance and grace, and is often referred to as a beauty in an echoing valley(幽谷美人). Because there are so many varieties, at least one will be in bloom at any given time of the year. One of the more poignant quotes of Confucius was "To be a friend with a true gentleman is like staying in a house filled with the fragrance of orchids. After a time, one notes not the fragrance, because it is intrinsically present."(与善人居，如入芝兰之室，久而不闻其香，即与之化矣。)That is to say, if one befriends a gentleman, one becomes a gentleman.

The great master of calligraphy, Wang Xizhi, built a pavilion named Orchid on Mt Kuaiji(会稽山的兰亭). He invited 42 respected scholars to the pavilion to drink wine and engage in a poetic jam session. He then collected these poems for a book, *The Collection of the Orchid Pavilion*(《兰亭集》)and wrote a preface to it. This piece of writing is highly respected for both its prose and the high aesthetic value of its running script calligraphy. In successive dynasties, many more poets wrote about or artistically expressed the orchid's beauty and grace. A powerful image painted at the turn of the Song and Yuan dynasties showed an orchid surviving without soil. The artist, Zheng Sixiao(郑思肖), was using this metaphor to convey that although the Yuan Dynasty took over, he would remain loyal to the Song Dynasty.

In late autumn, when hoar frost has already formed and the temperatures in the early morning dip below freezing, the chrysanthemum flourishes. It is regarded by Chinese people as strong, graceful, and with no egotistical desire for fame or gain. To indicate high-minded loftiness, the poet Qu Yuan of the State of Chu once wrote:

In the morning I drink water off fallen magnolia petals,
In the evening I have fallen chrysanthemum petals as sustenance.
(朝饮木兰之坠露兮，夕餐秋菊之落英。)

Tao Yuanming of the Eastern Jin Dynasty expressed his deep love for this flower through his poem:

While picking chrysanthemum beneath the eastern fence,

My gaze upon the southern mountain rests.

(采菊东离下，悠然见南山。)

A tranquil, peaceful scene to be sure! Over time many other poets have written about how the chrysanthemum flourishes in autumn, and maintains its delicate scent despite the cold wind attempting to sweep it away. For Chinese people, these are values to be held in high esteem.

Peony is another flower prized in Chinese culture. It is enjoyed for its stately color and heavenly fragrance(国色天香). Due to its grace and poise, it is a fitting symbol of splendor, wealth, and happiness. Among others, it was proposed as the national flower of China.

The most highly regarded classical piece of writing about peony is *Notes on Peony in Luoyang City*(《洛阳牡丹记》). This was written by Ouyang Xiu, a Song Dynasty man of letters. He elaborated on peony's history, methods of planting, varieties, and related customs. Literary figures of the Song and Ming dynasties also composed similar works. Liu Yuxi of the Tang Dynasty wrote a poem *Admiring Peony*(《赏牡丹》):

Compared to other flowers,

Peony is the only to possess stately beauty.

It touches everyone in the capital city

Where it blooms.

(唯有牡丹真国色,花开时节动京城。)

There is a legend that describes how peony came to be associated with the city of Luoyang. The Empress Wu Zetian planned to visit her Upper Garden(上苑) in early spring. At the time, the plants were budding but not yet in bloom. The fussy monarch issued an imperial decree in the form of a poem:

I will visit the Upper Garden tomorrow,

Spring shall be let known in time.

All flowers shall overnight bloom and grow

And wait not for vernal wind.

(明朝游上苑,火速报春知。花须连夜发,莫待晓风吹。)

The Empress had her wish — almost. Although the other flowers did as commanded, peony declined, due to its pride. Wu Zetian was furious and ordered peony be demoted to Luoyang. Peony has been endowed with the quality of indifference to the powerful and the influential, and strength to stay true to its own principles.

15.3.2 Cultural Implications of Animals

Animal is man's best friend. Different animals have different natural instincts and life styles. During the long-term intimate contact with animals, people have the deep-rooted understandings towards them. And the Chinese people and English people nearly have the same knowledge of animals' natural instincts and ways of life.

For example, English people would say, "He is as sly as a fox. He's foxy, and you've got to watch him." Chinese people would at once understand the meaning of the sentences as in Chinese, 他像狐狸一样狡猾，他很狡猾，你得注意点. This example indicates that *fox* can be used to describe someone who is cunning and deceitful. This example states that different languages and cultures endow *fox* the same associative meaning.

The following animal vehicles have the same associative meanings both in English and in Chinese. Donkey can be regarded as a kind of animal with dopey and stubborn temper. So *donkey* is used to show the character with obstinate and stupid temper both in English and in Chinese, e.g., as stubborn as a donkey (像驴一样固执).

Birds can fly to any place they like to. No wonder they are the embodiment of freedom in both English and Chinese. For example: "Bring the child down to me for a fortnight. I have a huge old garden where he can be as free as a bird and perfectly safe." Parrot is a kind of bird that can imitate people's sound. Both English people and Chinese people use *parrot* to refer to those who repeat someone else's words and ideas without really understanding what they hear, e.g., He just parrots what other people say (他只会鹦鹉学舌).

Pig or swine is used to describe such characteristics as dirty, greedy and lazy. For example, make a pig of oneself (贪婪地/狼吞虎咽地吃喝); He has been a pig about money. (他对钱贪得无厌。)

Because of different cultural, historical and traditional background, English people and Chinese people would have different associative meanings towards some animal vehicles.

Dog is a distinctive example in the two cultures. 狗 is very pejorative in meaning in Chinese. This can be readily illustrated by the Chinese words and idiomatic expressions in which it is an element: 走狗，丧家犬，狗头军师，狗急跳墙，狗腿子. In English culture, however, the dog is a pet, which can even be considered a family member. For example, there are three faithful friends: an old wife, an old dog and ready money. (人有三个忠实的朋友：老妻、老狗和现金。) It is hard for English speakers to understand why 走狗 is a pejorative term in Chinese. To them a dog is lovely and a running dog is doubly lovely. "Dog" and "狗" convey the same conceptual meaning, but their connotations are quite different in English and Chinese cultures.

In English culture, *owl* is symbolized of wisdom. *As wise as an owl* indicates that English people associate wisdom with this bird. In children's books and cartoons, the owl implies calmness and solemnity. For example, *He peers owlishly at us through his glasses*; *A tenant offering five bales of cotton was told, after some owl-eyed figuring, that this cotton exactly balanced his debt*. However, there is a superstitious belief that owl is an unlucky bird and is the symbol of disaster and death in Chinese people's minds, as the Chinese saying goes, 猫头鹰进宅,好事不来.

In Chinese, especially in ancient times, people thought dragon is a mythical animal with great power. To the Chinese, a dragon is something sacred and has been referred to as the ancestor of the Chinese nation. Chinese idioms that involve the word 龙 with good connotations are great in number: 龙腾虎跃, 龙生龙/凤生凤, 龙凤呈祥, 生龙活虎. Many Chinese would say 望子成龙, but its literal translation *to expect one's son to become a dragon* would sound ridiculous to English people. In western people's minds, the dragon is a large imaginary animal with wings and a long tail and can breathe out fire. To the westerners, the dragon is often a symbol of evil, a fierce and destructive monster. There is an example from *Collins Cobuild English Language Dictionary*: If you call a woman a dragon, you mean that she is fierce and unpleasant.

In Chinese people's eyes, *bat* means *auspicious* because 蝠 and 福 are homophonous. To English people, however, the bat is annoying and ugly and connected with evil and darkness. Therefore, in English, expressions with *bat* have derogatory meanings such as *as blind as a bat* and *as crazy as a bat*.

Chinese people give preference to the petrel(海燕) as a bird that braves the storm to fly over the vast ocean. So petrel is associated in China with courage and ordeal. The petrel emerges in many juvenile diaries, youthful fictional writings, and appears as the trademark for a number of products. However, English people do not like the bird, because they think petrel is the symbol for disasters, for when a storm is arising, petrel will flush, flying like lightening between black clouds and the sea. For example, *storm petrel* means a person regarded as a herald of trouble, strife or violence or someone who delights in such trouble, etc.

To Chinese people, tiger is a big and powerful carnivorous animal that is called the king of the beasts, so tiger is the symbol of courage, vigor, decisiveness and power, e. g., 虎虎有生气, 虎头虎脑,虎将 etc. In contrast, English people consider that the king of the beasts is lion, and lion is the symbol of courage, ferocity, dignity of dominance, as can be seen from such expressions as *regal as a lion*, *majestic as a lion*. The lion in the English culture enjoys high prestige. Richard I, King of England in the latter part of the 12th century, was known as lion-hearted for his courage and chivalry. When someone is called a lion, he is referred to a celebrity or a famous person. Therefore, there is another idiom *a lion-hunter*, which means a host or hostess who seeks out celebrities with whom to impress their guests. It's no wonder, then, that the English have chosen *the lion* as their symbol as in the expression *the British lion*. The word has been used to form many English idioms with such connotations. For instance, *lion's share* means the largest part; *the lion's den* means a place of great danger; *to meet a lion in one's path* means to encounter a daunting obstacle, etc.

15.4 Samples

爱莲说

On Loving the Lotus

周敦颐（宋）

Zhou Dun Yi of the Song Dynasty

水陆草木之花，可爱者甚蕃。

Among the flowers of water, land, herb and wood, many are loveable.

晋陶渊明独爱菊，自李唐来世人甚爱牡丹。

During Jin times Tao Yuan-Ming loved only the chrysanthemum, and since the Tang times people have greatly loved the peony.

予独爱莲之出淤泥而不染，濯清涟而不妖。

I love only the lotus for rising from the mud but is not stained, bathed by clear waves but is not seductive.

中通外直，不蔓不枝，香远益清，亭亭净植，

Inside, it is open; outside, it is straight. It neither crawls nor forks. The farther away one is, the purer is the fragrance. Upright and elegant, it establishes itself cleanly.

可远观而不可亵玩焉。

It can be viewed from far away but cannot be toyed with.

予谓菊，花之隐逸者也，

I say: the chrysanthemum is the recluse among flowers,

牡丹，花之富贵者也，莲，花之君子者也。

The peony is the wealthy among flowers, and the lotus is the gentleman among flowers.

噫，菊之爱，陶后鲜有闻，

Aye, the love for the chrysanthemum is seldom heard of after Tao.

莲之爱，同予者何人？

As for the love for the lotus, is there anyone like me?

牡丹之爱，宜乎众矣。

Ah, the love for the peony is right for most people.

卜算子·咏梅

Plum Blossom

陆游（宋）

Lu You of the Song Dynasty

驿外断桥边，

Near the broken bridge outside the fortress,
寂寞开无主。
I go, lonely and disoriented.
已是黄昏独自愁，
It is dusk and I am alone and anxious,
更著风和雨。
Especially in the blast of wind and rain.
无意苦争春，
I do not mean to fight for springtime,
一任群芳妒。
I would rather be alone and envied by the crowd.
零落成泥碾作尘，
I will fall down, become earth, be crushed to dust.
只有香如故。
My glory will be same as before.

15.5 A Glossary of Flora and Fauna in English and Chinese

Flora

桉树 eucalytus
八仙花 hydrangea
白桦 birch
白杨 poplar
百合花 lily
柏树 cypress
雏菊 marguerite, daisy
大丽花 dahlia
大树枝 bough
大竺葵 geranium
倒挂金钟 fuchsia
丁香 lilac
冬青 holly
杜鹃花 azalea
杜鹃花 rhododendron
杜松 juniper
风信花 hyacinth
枫树 maple
凤仙花 balsam

海棠花 Chinese flowering crab-apple
黑刺李 blackthorn
红杉 sequoia
蝴蝶花 fringed iris
黄水仙 daffodil
黄杨 box
夹竹桃 oleander
接骨木 elder
金盏花 marigold
菊花 chrysanthemum
橘子 orange
康乃馨 carnation
兰花 orchid
冷杉 fir
梨 pear
龙舌兰 cantury plant
落叶松 larch
曼陀罗 datura
美人蕉 canna
木槿 hibiscus
牵牛花 morning-glory
秋海棠 begonia
瑞香 daphne
山茶花 camellia
山毛榉 beech
山楂 hawthorn
山茱萸 dogwood
芍药 peony
树皮 bark
水仙花 narcissus
松 pine
松果 cone
昙花 epiphyllum
乌檀 ebony
仙人掌 cactus
仙人掌 night-blooming cereus
向日葵 sunflower
橡树 oak

杏 apricot
雪松 cerdar
洋槐 locust
椰树 coco
银杏树 ginkgo
罂粟花 poppy
油棕榈树 oil palm
柚木树 teak
榆木树 elm
玉兰花 mangnolia
郁金香 tulip
云杉 spruce
枣树 date
樟树 camphor tree
栀子 gardenia
紫荆 redbud
紫檀 rosewood

Fauna
矮马 pony
长臂猿 gibbon
雌猫 catta
雌山羊 nanny
雌猪 sow
刺猬 hedgehog
大猩猩 gorilla
单峰驼 dromedary
海豹 seal
海象 walrus
河狸 beaver
河马 hippopotamus
河豚 dolphin
黑猩猩 chimpanzee
箭猪，豪猪 porcupine
鬣狗 hyena
羚羊 antelope
马驹，小马 colt，foal
牦牛 yak

美洲豹 panther，puma
美洲野牛 bison
猞猁 lynx
食蚁兽 anteater
树懒 sloth
水牛 buffalo
水獭 otter
睡鼠 dormouse
田鼠 vole
土拨鼠 marmot
犀牛 rhinoceros
小火鸡 poult
小羚羊 gazelle
小猫 kitten
小母猪 gilt
小牛，牛犊 calf
小阉牛 bullock，steer
小羊驼 vicuna
猩猩 orangutan
雄鹅 gander
雄火鸡 tom
雄马 stallion
雄猫 tomcat
雄绵羊 ram
雄牛 bull，ox
雄猪 boar
雪貂 ferret
驯鹿 reindeer
鸭嘴兽 duckbill，platypus
阉马 gelding
阉猪，肥猪 hog
鼹鼠 mole
羊驼 alpaca
野马 mustang
鼬，黄鼠狼 weasel

Chapter 16 Contrast of Sino-Western Cultures and Chinese-English Translation Texts in the Field of Food and Cuisine

16.1 What Are Food and Cuisine

Food is any substance consumed to provide nutritional support for the body. It is usually of plant or animal origin, and contains essential nutrients, such as fats, proteins, vitamins, or minerals. The substance is ingested by an organism and assimilated by the organism's cells to provide energy, maintain life, or stimulate growth.

Most food has its origin in plants. Some food is obtained directly from plants; even animals that are used as food sources are fed by food derived from plants.

Some foods not obtained from animal or plant sources include various edible fungi, especially mushrooms. Fungi and ambient bacteria are used in the preparation of fermented and pickled foods like leavened (加酵母的) bread, alcoholic drinks, cheese, pickles, kombucha, and yogurt. Another example is blue-green algae (藻类) such as spirulina (螺旋藻属). Inorganic substances such as salt, baking soda and cream of tartar (酒石) are used to preserve or chemically alter an ingredient.

A cuisine is a style of cooking characterized by distinctive ingredients, techniques and dishes, and usually associated with a specific culture or geographic region. A cuisine is primarily influenced by the ingredients that are available locally or through trade. Religious food laws, such as Hindu, Islamic and Jewish dietary laws, can also exercise a strong influence on cuisine. Regional food preparation traditions, customs and ingredients often combine to create dishes unique to a particular region.

16.2 Cultural Contrast of Food and Cooking in China and the West

16.2.1 Food and Cooking in China

Rice is a major staple food for people from rice farming areas in southern China. Steamed rice, usually white rice, is the most commonly eaten form. Rice is also used to produce beers, wines and vinegars. Rice is one of the most popular foods in China and is used in many dishes. Glutinous rice (sticky rice) is a variety of rice used in many specialty Chinese dishes.

Chinese noodles come dry or fresh in a variety of sizes, shapes and textures and are often served in soups or fried as toppings. Some varieties, such as Shou Mian (literally noodles of longevity), are symbolic of long life and good health according to Chinese tradition. Noodles can be served hot or cold with different toppings, with broth, and occasionally dry. Noodles are commonly made with rice flour or wheat flour, but other flours such as soybean are also used.

Tofu is made of soybeans and is another popular food product that supplies protein. Other products such as soy milk, soy paste, soy oil, and fermented soy sauce are also important in Chinese cooking.

In wheat-farming areas in northern China, people largely rely on flour-based food, such as noodles, breads, jiaozi (a kind of Chinese dumplings), and mantou (a type of steamed buns).

In larger cities, a wide variety of Chinese bakery products are available, including baked, steamed, boiled, or deep-fried sweet or savory snacks. Bings(饼) are baked wheat flour based confections (糕点), and include moon cake, red bean paste pancake, and sun cake (太阳饼). Chinese candies and sweets are usually made with cane sugar, malt sugar, honey, nuts and fruit. Gao(糕) is rice-based snack that is typically steamed and may be made from glutinous or normal rice.

Chinese tea is often classified into several different categories according to the species of plant from which it is sourced, the region in which it is grown, and the method of production. Some are green tea, oolong tea, black tea, scented tea, white tea, and compressed tea. There are four major tea plantation regions: Jiangbei, Jiangnan, Huanan and the southwestern region. Well known types of green tea include Longjing, Huangshan, Mao Feng, Biluochun, Putuofengcha, and Liu'an Guapian. China is the world's largest exporter of green tea.

Chinese food not only has a reputation of being delicious, it is also considered an art form in its own right. Chinese cuisine involves looking at the combination of the ingredients as well as paying particular attention to the complex process and equipment involved. Different ingredients are cooked using different methods, while the same ingredient can be used in different dishes to provide different flavors and appearances. There are hundreds of cuisines in China. However, the most common methods are stir-frying (炒), deep-frying (炸), shallow-frying (煎), braising(炖), boiling (煮), steaming (蒸) and roasting (烤). The following is a detailed introduction.

1. Stir-frying

The most frequently used method is stir-frying. This method cooks processed ingredients at high heat for a short period of time. Edible oil is used as the heat conductor. Usually, a wok(锅) is used at high heat, edible oil is added followed by ingredients and seasonings. Due to the short period of time involved in the process, ingredients largely keep their nutritional value. Stir-fried meat is typically juicy and tasty, and vegetables are usually tender and crispy.

2. Deep-frying

Deep-frying uses much more edible oil than stir-frying (the ingredient should be fully submerged in the oil), producing crisp-textured food. The common method of preparing deep-frying dishes is to cut the ingredients into medium-sized pieces or chunks, soak them in prepared seasoning for a while, coat with corn starch (optional), and finally fry in hot deep oil over medium heat. The density of coating will determine the levels of crispness and tenderness on the inside and outside of the ingredients used.

3. Shallow-frying

As the name implies, shallow-frying is a cuisine using less edible oil than deep-frying and lower heat than stir-frying. Shallow-fried dishes are usually rather tender inside, appearing golden or slightly burnt outside. The ingredients for shallow-frying are usually cut into slices or flat pieces and rubbed with seasonings. To make the outer skin crispy, the ingredients are also slightly coated with corn starch after being seasoned. When cooking, the ingredients should be shallow-fried on one side first and then turned to the other.

4. Braising

To cook large-sized ingredients melt-in-your-mouth, braising is to add ingredients and seasonings in a wok or a saucepan at the same time, add in some water, boil it and then simmer it for one hour or more. The ingredients are usually cut into cubes or diamonds. To cook dishes by braising, the ingredients especially the animal ingredients should be scalded in boiling water and rinsed in clean water first to get rid of the fishy smell, and the sauce is thickened either with corn starch or reduced by simmering finally.

5. Boiling

Boiling could be considered the simplest among all the Chinese cuisines. It simply involves placing food in boiling water. It is mainly used for cooking small-sized and soft ingredients, especially for most of the vegetable soups like tomato and egg soup and tofu soup. Prepared ingredients are placed into a wok, along with water and appropriate seasonings when the surface of the water is continually agitated by large bubbles. Dishes cooked by boiling always taste fresh and clear, for it takes a shorter time than braising.

6. Steaming

A special cuisine invented in China is steaming. It is widely used for steaming buns and dumplings in northern China, where people live on wheaten food. The process involves placing the ingredients in a steamer basket which is placed over water in a steamer pot. Steamed food contains more nutrition than boiled food for less nutrition is leached into the water. Very little edible oil and fewer seasonings are used, so the food's natural flavor is maintained and even enhanced.

7. Roasting

Roasting is to cook the food over the open flame of charcoal or in an oven. The moisture of the food is removed while seasonings are rubbed in from the outside. The outside of the roasted food always gets drier and browned, but flavors are retained and enhanced. Many ingredients can be roasted, including all kinds of meat along with most root and bulb vegetables. To roast food, the ingredients must be cleaned, seasoned and basted with edible oil in order to reduce the loss of moisture in the ingredients during the roasting process.

16.2.2 Food and Cooking in the West

British cuisine is the specific set of cooking traditions and practices associated with the United Kingdom. British cuisine has been described as "unfussy dishes made with quality local ingredients, matched with simple sauces to accentuate flavour, rather than disguise it." However, British cuisine has absorbed the cultural influence of those who have settled in Britain, producing many hybrid dishes, such as the Anglo-Indian chicken tikka masala (烤鸡咖喱).

Anglo-Saxon England developed meat and savory herb stewing techniques before the practice became common in Europe. The Norman conquest introduced exotic spices into England in the Middle Ages. The British Empire facilitated a knowledge of India's elaborate food tradition of "strong, penetrating spices and herbs." Food rationing policies, put in place by the British government during wartime periods of the 20th century, are said to have been the stimulus for British cuisine's poor international reputation. It has been claimed, contrary to popular belief, that people in southern England eat more garlic per head than people of northern France.

British cuisine has traditionally been limited in its international recognition to the full breakfast, fish and chips, and the Christmas dinner. Other British dishes include the Sunday roast, steak and kidney pie, shepherd's pie, and bangers and mash. British cuisine has many regional varieties within the broader categories of English, Scottish and Welsh cuisine. Each has developed its own regional or local dishes, many of which are geographically indicated foods such as Cornish pasties, the Yorkshire pudding, Cumberland Sausage, Arbroath Smokie, and Welsh cakes.

Food of the United States reflects its history. The European colonization of the Americas yielded the introduction of a number of ingredients and cooking styles to the latter. The various styles continued expanding well into the 19th and 20th centuries, proportional to the influx of immigrants from many foreign nations; such influx developed a rich diversity in food preparation throughout the country.

When the colonists came to the colonies, they farmed animals for clothing and meat in a similar fashion to what they had done in Europe. They had food similar to their previous British food. The American colonial diet varied depending on the settled region in which someone lived. Commonly hunted game included deer, bear, buffalo, and wild turkey. A number of fats and oils made from animals served to cook much of the colonial food. Prior to the Revolution, New Englanders consumed large quantities of rum and beer, as maritime trade provided them relatively easy access to the goods needed to produce these items: rum was the distilled spirit of choice, as the main ingredient, molasses(糖蜜), was readily available from trade with the West Indies. In comparison to the northern colonies, the southern colonies were quite diverse in their agricultural diet and did not have a central region of culture.

16.3 Chinese-English Translation Texts in the Field of Food and Cuisine

16.3.1 Supplementing Cultural Background in the Source Language

The Chinese is a nation of good food. But in translating the names of food literal translation often fails because many foods have beautiful stories behind them.

佛跳墙 (Buddha jumping over the wall): It is a good food, and yet it has nothing to do with but is offensive to the faith of Buddhism. In introducing this food readers will not be satisfied unless the whole story is brought forth: It is the chief traditional dish in Ju ChunYuan Restaurant. It is stewed with more than twenty kinds of ingredients including shark's fin, sea-cucumber scallop(扇贝); abalone fish maw(鲍鱼鱼肚), etc. The cooking procedure is very strict. The ingredients are well-selected and cutting is also quite an art. It tastes mellow and tender.

贵妃鸡 (Highest-ranking imperial concubine chicken): Stewed chicken invented in Qing Dynasty and named after Lady Yang who was the highest-ranking imperial concubine in Tang Dynasty.

叫化子鸡(Beggar's chicken): Toasted in lotus leaf and earth mud, invented by two beggars in Qing Dynasty.

麻婆豆腐(Mapo's tofu): Stir-fried tofu in hot sauce.

东坡肉(Braised pork): Invented by Su Dongpo who was a famous poet in Song Dynasty.

宫保鸡丁(Diced chicken with chili and peanuts in hot sauce): Invented by Gongbao in Qing Dynasty.

金玉满堂(A house filled with gold and jade): Assorted barbecued meat platter with portion of crispy barbecued suckling pig.

16.3.2 Discriminating Semantic Nuances Between Tricky Synonyms

English and Chinese have many near synonyms for cuisine, negligence of the semantic nuances will ruin the cuisine in the other language if the recipe is translated on this basis. Examples of near synonyms are cited below.

Simmer, *stew*, *braise*, *curry*, *poach* have much in common with 焖、煨、扒、煲, since both groups require a big consumption of water, mild fire, comparatively long time, etc, but they are not the same procedures of cuisine. Stew, braise and 焖 are more close to each other because the cooking pot has to be covered in this process. Braise applies for the preparation of meat. Simmer and 煨 are better synonyms. 焖, 煨, 扒 use less oil while *simmer*, *stew*, *poach* do not use oil. Poach is the processing of fish and egg, while *curry* requires the use of curry powder, hence no counterpart in Chinese. 扒 means excessive cooking, 煲 requires a special cooking pot not available outside China.

Fry, sauté, frizzle and 炸、煎、熘、爆、炒、煸、煌、炮、烹 are near synonyms, while fry, sauté, frizzle resort to flat pots, but their Chinese near synonyms do not. In sauting cream is used, but Chinese has no equivalent for *sauté*. 爆, 炒, 煸, 煌, 炮, 烹 involve frequent stirring, so they are vacant in English.

Bake and 烙 are close to each other. The act of baking is done in an oven, while 烙 is done in a flat pot.

Roast, baste and 煨 are close. Hot ashes are used in these processes, but for the cuisine of roasting, open fire will be suitable apart from hot ashes. In roasting and basting, the dripping lard is collected and put back to the meat together with cream or soybean sauce.

Broil, grill, barbecue, charcoal, plank, toast, sear, scallop have no equivalents in Chinese, while 烧, 烩, 酿, 摊, 焯, 涮, 烫, 汆, 炖, 冲, 烘, 酱, 腌, 泡 do not have ready synonyms in English.

16.4 Samples

First we are to introduce some Chinese snacks or their preparation methods, and then we shall introduce some British snacks.

Let's come to some delicious Chinese snacks first:

麻辣烫 Malatang(numb, spicy soup): You pick your own skewered vegetables and meat from the shelf before you ask the staff to boil them together in chicken or pork broth.

生煎包 Sheng jian (fried bun): Fried and garnished with fresh spring onion and toasted sesame. They taste best just out of the pan — totally worth the blisters on your tongue.

豆腐花 Tofu soup: Made by curdling soy milk, this smooth tofu soup contains the subtle flavor of soybeans beneath a colorful mixed dressing of dried shrimps, pickled radish, seaweed, scallion, soy sauce and chili oil.

烤红薯 Baked sweet potato: Sweet, fluffy, and fibrous, usually sold out of a pushcart, they are one of the healthiest snacks in town.

凉皮 Cold jelly noodles: Stir up the chunky, chewy jelly noodles and fresh vegetables with sesame sauce, vinegar, and chili oil, and then sprinkle some toasted peanuts and sesame for the final touch.

British snacks abound:

Fish and chips: A hot dish of English origin consisting of fried battered fish and hot chips. It is a common take-away food and an early example of culinary fusion. First appearing in the 1860s, in 1910 there were more than 25,000 fish and chip shops across the UK, and by the 1930s it increased to over 35,000.

Aero: Chocolate filled with air bubbles and it comes in various flavours. The mint one is vividly green and it's the best.

Flakes: Just chocolate but they fall apart more in your mouth. We have a tradition of sticking it in soft serve ice cream. This is called a 99 or a Mr Whippy.

Tea cakes: Filled with the fluffiest marshmallow and chewy caramel wafers.

Smarties: Look like chocolate but aren't chocolate at all, they taste a bit like refreshers.

16.5 A Glossary of Food and Cuisines in English and Chinese

Food or unprepared materials:

八角 star anise

白花菜 cauliflower

包心菜 white cabbage

比目鱼 plaice

冰糖 rock sugar

菠菜 spinach

薄荷 mint

糙米 brown rice

草莓 strawberry

醋 vinegar
大白菜 Chinese leaves
大葱 leek
大红豆 red kidney bean
大茴香，八角，大料 anise (star anise)
大茴香子 aniseed
大块牛排 rump steak
大蒜 garlic
大芋头 taro
丁香 clove
豆腐 tofu
豆豉 salt black bean
方便面 instant noodles
鲱鱼 herring
粉丝 vermicelli
腐皮 beancurd sheet
鲑鱼 salmon
海带 sea vegetable or sea weed
海鳗 conger (eel)
蚝油 oyster sauce
黑豆 black bean
黑香肠 black pudding
红豆 red bean
红枣 red date
胡椒 pepper
胡萝卜 carrot
花椒 Chinese red pepper
黄瓜 cucumber
茴香 fennel
鸡腿 chicken drumsticks
姜 ginger
酱油 soy sauce
芥末 mustard
苦艾 wormwood
辣椒，牛角椒 cayenne pepper
辣椒 chilli
辣椒粉 red chilli powder
鲤鱼 carp

荔枝 lychee
龙虾 lobster
绿豆 green bean
绿豆芽 bean sprouts
绿花菜 broccoli
麻油 sesame oil
马铃薯 potato
麦芽糖 maltose
芒果 mango
蜜瓜 honeydew melon
面条 noodle
牡蛎 oyster
柠檬 lemon
牛腱肉 leg beef
牛筋 cowhells
糯米 glutinous rice
螃蟹 crab
葡萄 grape
奇异果 kiwi
芹菜 celery
青椒 green pepper
秋葵 okra
肉桂 cinnamon
砂糖(泡奶茶、咖啡适用)brown sugar
四季豆 dwarf bean
蹄膀 hock
田螺 winkle
豌豆 pea
莴苣 lettuce
乌贼 squid
虾 prawn
虾米 dried shrimp
虾仁 peeled prawn
香菜 coriander
香辣椒,多香果,牙买加胡椒 allspice
香叶,月桂树叶 bay leaf
小豆蔻 cardamom
小虾米 shrimp

鳕鱼 cod
鳕鱼子 cod roe
熏鲑鱼 smoked salmon
熏肉 smoked meat，bacon
燕菜 agaragar
杨桃 star fruit
洋葱 onion
腰果 cashew nut
椰油 creamed coconut
椰子 coconut
樱桃 cherry
鱼干 dried fish
月桂 laurel
章鱼 octopus
芝麻籽 sesame seed
芝麻酱 sesame paste
猪油 lard
孜然，小茴香，枯茗 cumin

Cuisines：
冲泡/煮 brew (prepare a drink，such as tea，by infusing)
氽烫 blanch (dip quickly into very hot water；for example carrots)
捣成泥 mash (convert into soft pulpy mixture as in mashed potatoes)
炖 simmer (cook over a low flame after coming to the boil)
翻面 toss (mix a salad lightly so as to cover with dressing)
烘焙(面食类)bake (cook in the oven；for example bread)
烘烤 toast (heat and brown in a toaster，oven or near a fire；for example bread)
烘烤(肉类) roast (cook with dry heat，especially in an oven；for example duck)
绞碎 mince (chop，cut or grind into very small pieces)
搅拌 whip (beat rapidly to force air into a mixture，as in whipped cream)
焖 stew(cook for a long time over a low flame)
磨碎 grate (shred food，such as carrots or cheese，with a grater)
泡入卤汁 marinate (soak，especially meat，in spiced liquid or wine，usually overnight)
切丝 shred (cut into long and thin pieces)
切小块 dice (chop into cubes)
揉面 knead (work dough with the hands，before baking in the oven to make bread)

(用烤架)烤 grill (cook by direct heat as in a barbecue or under a grill)

油煎、炒 sauté (cook in a small amount of oil until brown)

油炸 fry (cook in hot oil)

蒸 steam (place food over boiling water so that it cooks in the steam)

煮 boil (cook in hot, boiling water)